John Lyons' The Making of a Perfect Horse

Perfectly Practical
Advice on

Horsemanship

ISBN: 1-879-620-60-X

Please note: The information appearing in this publication is presented for educational purposes only. In no case shall the publishers or authors be held responsible for any use readers may choose to make, or not to make, of this information.

Belvoir Publications Inc.
Box 2626
75 Holly Hill Lane
Greenwich, CT 06836 USA

Lyons. John
Perfectly Practical Advice on Horsemanship
Lyons, John, Kellon, Eleanor V.M.D.
and the editors of John Lyons' Perfect Horse

ISBN: 1-879-620-60-X
1. Horses - Training   2. Horsemanship   3. Horses

Manufactured in the United States of America

John Lyons' The Making of a Perfect Horse

Perfectly Practical
Advice on

Horsemanship

John Lyons with Maureen Gallatin,
Eleanor Kellon V.M.D.
and the editors of John Lyons' Perfect Horse

Belvoir Publications, Inc.
Greenwich, CT

Contents

Section II: Practical Advice about Riding

Preface

The words "perfect" and "practical" may not seem to go together when talking about riding and horsekeeping advice, until you remember that neither riding nor horsekeeping are exact sciences. No matter how hard we try to "get it right," variables exist that keep us "just doing the best we can." But the best we can do isn't second rate, it's what God expects from us in an imperfect world.

In this book, we'll cover important topics such as how horses interact with each other, but then we'll make that information practical by telling you how to introduce a new horse to the herd without anyone getting kicked. The better you understand how your horse thinks and acts, the better you can get along with him. That doesn't mean becoming part of his herd; it means teaching him to interact in our world. Along those lines, we'll detail important lessons such as teaching your foal to lead and the practical — but we-wish-we-didn't-have-to-deal-with-it — topic of bucking. None of that falls into the "Put Tab A Into Slot B" category but neither is it the kind of information we should take for granted.

Living with horses successfully requires that we filter all we learn through a common-sense grid, that we think of our perfect horses practically and that we integrate what we've learned from all areas of life. God never intended for us to compartmentalize life, but to bring to all our relationships the best of what we have to offer — and that includes the relationship with our perfect horse.

Trust in the Lord with all your heart; do not depend on your own understanding. Seek His will in all you do, and He will direct your path.
Proverbs 3: 5,6

Section I

Perfectly Practical
Advice About
Horsekeeping

1

"Give" To Pressure, Please

*This may be one of the most important lessons
you ever teach your foal — or your adult horse
if he didn't learn it when he was young.*

When you see a horse dragging someone at the end of the lead rope, what part of the horse's training is missing? When a horse pulls back on the cross ties or can't be tied in the trailer, what lesson did he not learn? And when a horse panics because he stepped on his rein, what could we have taught him to prevent a wreck? The answers to those questions are all the same — give to pressure. By "give to pressure" we mean that when the horse feels a pull from a lead rope he should move in the direction of the pull, rather than brace against the pull.

If the first horse had been taught to give to pressure, he would not have pulled on his handler. If the second horse had learned this lesson, when he felt pressure on his head, he would have moved forward and toward where he was tied, thus relieving the pressure. And when the third horse felt pressure on the bit, he would have moved his head down toward his foot to relieve the pressure instead of raising his head, feeling trapped and snapping the rein.

Now imagine how much different a horse's life would be if he learned to give to pressure as a foal. You'd save him many fearful moments and yourself much frustration, and you might just save yourself and your horse from injury. **Instead of the horse feeling that he has to flee or fight when he is restrained, he'll learn that rather than resisting the pressure, if he moves in the other direction, he'll feel a release.** Once he learns this concept, it will stand him in good stead throughout his life.

Round-pen training for foals reviewed

John started out with the first round-pen objective — he got the foal's feet to move. He went around one side of the mare. Naturally, the foal went around to the other side.

Building on that, he established a pattern of asking the foal's feet to move, by directing body language to a spot on the top of the foal's hip. With repetition, the foal understood that meant he should walk a few steps forward.

When the foal tried to double back, John continued to ask him to go forward — getting the feet to move consistently. Next it was a matter of getting the foal's feet to move in the desired direction. So, by focusing on the

*foal's nose and gently blocking his path, John began ask-
ing the foal to change directions. As soon as the foal
began to turn, John stepped away to allow the foal to complete the turn, and he focused on the foal's hip, telling
him to move his feet as he did in the beginning steps.*

*When the turn to the right was perfected, he worked on
turning to the left. Then, by shortening the distance
between the right and left turns, John taught the foal to
look toward him. When the foal did what John wanted,
he stepped away, rewarding the foal's good effort. All this
was done at the walk, with occasional trot steps.*

*Next John sacked the foal out thoroughly, using the stan-
dard Lyons' sacking-out method. First petting, then stopping petting and walking away before the horse moves
away. Then he pet the foal with various objects, each
time withdrawing the object before the foal felt the need
to move. In that way, the foal learned that John was not
going to hurt him and that being handled was enjoyable.*

*Using the same sacking-out procedure, John draped the
halter over one ear, then the other, then up and down the
foal's muzzle. Eventually he taught the foal to drop his
nose into the halter on cue. John spent lots of time hug-
ging and stroking the foal so that he gained confidence.*

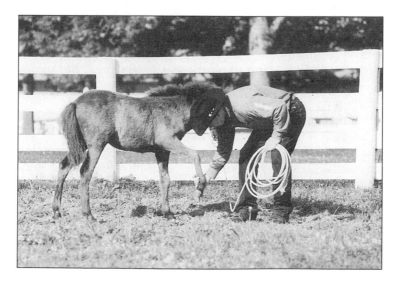

By the time you are ready to thread the lariat through the halter, neither the halter nor the lariat are foreign to the foal, but he should enjoy the attention.

How pulling and giving work

Imagine, for a moment, that you were holding the end of a rope. Someone pulls on the other end. Instinctively, you match him pull for pull. Horses respond that way instinctively, too. When, for instance, you try to lead a reluctant horse forward into a trailer, he may raise his head and resist your pull. **You pull on the lead rope, and the horse feels the pull on the top of his head, not under his chin where the lead is attached.**

Or when we pull on the left rein when riding, instead of the horse moving his head to the left, which would ease the pressure on the rein, his reaction is normally to lean to the right — pulling against the pull. And, if we've ever pushed on a horse's side, trying to make an untrained horse move over in the washrack, instead of stepping away from our push, he pushes against us.

We want to replace our horse's instinctive reaction with a learned response. When we push on his side in the washrack (and later when we use our leg on his side), we want him to step away. When we pull the left rein, we want him to turn his nose left. When we pull on the lead rope, we want the horse to put his head down or forward.

In this lesson, we will concentrate on teaching the horse to give to pressure on the halter.

We'll put very slight pressure on the lead rope. The moment the foal moves in the correct direction, we'll release the pressure, letting him know he made a good decision. **We use only light pressure initially because then he'll meet our light resistance with only light resistance.** If we used a lot of pressure, just like if someone pulled hard on that rope you were holding in our earlier example, he'd meet our pull with a lot of resistance, causing him to get scared and upset. **And horses don't learn when they are scared. Fear interferes with learning.**

How much pressure

Once the horse "gives" to light pressure, we'll add more and more resistance, so that he learns to give even if he gets jerked on. It's not that we ever want to jerk on him, but he's likely to hit the end of a rope hard and fast if he should get scared, and that's when we most want him to keep his cool.

There'll be a day when he's tied to the trailer and something startles him. He'll pull back hard at that moment, which is natural. If he's learned to give, he'll only hit the end of that rope for a moment, then step forward, preventing a wreck.

Or, let's say you have him ground tied, and he steps on his reins. When he goes to raise his head with his foot on the rein, he could feel a pretty hard pull on his poll. If he's been taught to give, he'll immediately drop his nose toward his foot and release himself from the pull of the reins. But that kind of response is the goal, not our starting point. So we'll begin with our foal by putting light pressure on the halter and expecting that he learns to move his head away from that pressure on his head, which is really toward the source of the pull.

Of course, with any lesson, three rules prevail: The trainer cannot get hurt; the horse cannot get hurt; and the horse should be calmer at the end of the lesson than at the beginning. Working with foals, a trainer must be exceptionally careful, because they frighten and tire easily. In addition to teaching this specific "give to pressure" lesson, we are conditioning our foal to get along with us, and that we are going to ask him a series of easy questions to which he can always answer yes. That will establish a foundation of cooperation that will last him a lifetime. Let's review the lessons we'll have done with our foal prior to teaching him to give to pressure.

With the foal haltered, review some of the round-pen steps you did earlier so the horse is in the pattern of moving away and then looking toward you. Because John sacked the foal out with the lariat, he isn't afraid of the lariat when John threads it through the halter ring (photo #1). **Be sure not to use a lead rope with a metal snap that could hurt or scare the foal.**

Next, John backs away from the foal and asks him to move forward going left, as he did in the initial round-pen lessons, focusing on the foal's left hip cue spot (photo #2). John walks along 10 to 15 feet behind the foal, letting the lariat hang as if it was not there at all.

After the foal relaxes, John slowly takes the slack out of the lariat until he has about three pounds of pressure on the line. When the foal slows his feet, questioning the pressure on the rope, John lets him stop. Then he releases the line and walks up to the foal, petting him to let him know that was what John wanted him to do.

In photo #3, the foal turned to face John when he put pressure on the lead. That is a "freebie," a response more advanced than the horse would normally do at this stage. It earns him a special "Good for you" (photo #4), but we won't assume he knew what he did to earn the reward. Nor will we assume he can repeat the maneuver.

After repeating the stop-when-you-feel-pressure routine a few times, John asked the foal to look toward him when he stopped. After releasing the lariat, he again put very light pressure on it until the foal looked at him. Then he released the line again as he walked up to pet the foal.

The next step was to keep the foal moving, but to have him bend his neck and look toward John (photos #5 and #6 on the next page). When the foal stops this time, John asks him to look toward him, but then he tells the foal to walk again. John moves closer to the foal, but continues the stop-and-start routine with the foal's neck bent toward John. If the foal stops on his own, John asks him to keep moving.

John didn't cue the foal to just look at him with the kiss or some other body language, because the objective was to teach the horse to give to pressure on the halter.

John continues the lesson along the same lines until he can walk almost beside the foal with the foal's neck bent slightly and until the foal will stop with light pressure on the line. **At no point will John pull the foal forward; he always drives the foal forward from the hip.**

When John can get the foal to move forward consistently, he'll work closer to the foal's shoulder — the normal leading position. There may be times when he asks the foal to move, and the foal moves a little quicker than he'd like. Then he'll adjust tension on the lariat so the foal doesn't "hit" the end of the line or pull on the lariat. You don't want him to learn to pull. (Note: Just as you can teach horses *not* to pull, you can teach them *to* pull. Calf-roping horses, for instance, learn to hold a rope taut. Unfortunately, many people inadvertently teach their riding horses to pull on the lead rope or rein.)

Once the foal walks along beside John easily and stops with light tension on the lariat, John will teach him to trot beside him, using the same lesson format. He'll begin with the foal walking about 15 feet in front of him, then he'll ask the foal to trot, cueing the same hip cue spot. **The faster the horse's feet are moving, the longer it**

may take to stop his feet and give to the pressure of the lariat. John won't increase the intensity of the pull; he'll just allow the foal a longer time to respond. If the foal gets excited, John will backtrack in the lesson, getting it down pat at the walk.

When the lesson is down pat and the foal will follow tension on the lead, you can gradually work up to teaching the foal to follow the pull when it comes from a different direction. In photo #7, John brings the rope around the back of the foal and pulls lightly, expecting the foal to turn right to follow the pull. (Because the earlier sacking-out lesson was done well, the foal isn't worried about the rope around his legs or hindquarters.) **Of course, as soon as the foal begins to turn in the correct direction, John will release tension on the rope. He'll also release the rope if the horse gets upset at any point.** No one response is worth getting the horse scared. John will just let the rope go and backtrack in the lesson until the foal is comfortable with the next step.

Let's see what was accomplished in this lesson. John taught the foal to move toward the tension on the line. He taught the foal to lead, without ever pulling on the lead rope. And the foal learned that education is a matter of the trainer asking questions and the foal getting loved on when he answers them correctly. Not a bad day's work. ▣

For more information about working with foals see COMMUNICATING WITH CUES PART III, VOLUME 4, JOHN LYONS PERFECT HORSE LIBRARY.

Notes

2

It's Instinctive

Horseowners sometimes find themselves wondering if a horse's actions are a result of his natural tendencies or caused by something the rider may have done.

Run first, ask questions later. That's the first law of being a horse. Upon encountering a scary object — like a bicyclist, a bird flushed from the bushes or the freshly placed potted flowers beside the arena — the horse will instinctively presume danger and hastily move away. **Pastured horses often run to a safe distance, then turn to look back at the threatening object.**

Even more scary are objects that "chase" the horse, such as the neighbor's dog, the noisy truck that comes up behind him on the road or the "dragon" (draggin') lead rope. These elicit the same run-for-your-life behavior, but since they "pursue" the horse (at least in his mind), the horse is unlikely to find a comfortable distance from which he can stop to investigate.

The horse becomes even more frantic in his attempts to get away when the scary object is attached to him, such as when your riding rain coat comes unsnapped. The faster he goes, the more wildly the coat flaps. **We know from our understanding of the horse's natural behavior never to chase — on foot or on horseback — a runaway horse. He'll just run faster. Hopefully, if you stop, he'll stop too, to look back and investigate.**

When a horse can't run, his next-best defense is to kick. Horses can kick out behind them or forward all the way up to their shoulder. The forward-reaching hind leg kick, called a cow kick, might be used by the horse who objects to his girth being tightened.

The forward motion of a front foot is called striking, and it is seen

When one horse starts running, the others in the pasture usually join him. And that may include the horse you're riding.

when horses meet each other, sniffing nose to nose, and one objects to the other's nearness. **Trained horses should not kick or strike at people.**

Horses can become desensitized to common objects like raincoats, flushed birds and barking dogs. But you cannot desensitize them to everything they'll encounter. The wise handler or rider will teach the horse to "spook in place." You can't tell the horse not to be afraid, but you can teach him what to do when he is afraid, and thus reduce the chances of injury to him or you.

Reading his ears

When the horse's ears are flat back against his neck, usually he's irritated and letting you know it. Like a dog growling, he's saying, "Get out of my way." We see this, for example, in cutting horses intent on a cow. This threat may be enough to get the other individual's attention — if the offending animal backs off, the threat may cease. Or, the ears laid flat back may be followed by a threatening swing of the head or a bite. The ears also sometimes go flat back during supreme effort, such as when a barrel racer heads for home.

When a rider communicates to the horse, either verbally or non-verbally, the horse will often flick one or both ears back in response.

For example, picking up the left rein will get the horse's attention, and you may see his left ear flick back toward you.

The horse rotates his ears to gather data, like you rotate a satellite dish to better catch the message. Both ears forward means he's investigating something out front. One ear forward and one ear back means his attention is divided. The horse's ears mirror his eye movements — so we can watch his ears to see what he's looking at.

Relaxed, tired or sleeping, the horse's ears hang idly to the side.

Sleep and sleep needs

A system of ligaments and tendons in the legs forms the "stay apparatus," which allows the horse to sleep standing up. This also has its roots in the wild, as it allows the horse to awaken quickly and sprint from danger. **Beware of startling a sleeping horse. He may react instinctively, jumping away from you or kicking out.**

A mature horse requires about 20 minutes of deep "rapid eye movement" (REM) sleep in each 24-hour period, during which he will likely lie down. The horse who stretches out on the warm, southern slope in the winter sun is probably catching up on his REM sleep, plus maximizing body area to absorb heat from the sun. **Deep-sleep deprivation can result in poor performance and the inability to "concentrate."**

The eyes have it

■ *Understanding the horse's vision helps us influence and predict his reactions. The horse can see to the front and nearly all the way behind him, on both sides, without moving his head. When he is not concentrating on an object to the front — when you see his ears doing anything other than both pointing straight ahead — he can take in sights on both sides, similar to our peripheral vision. This is called "monocular vision."*

When using monocular vision, the horse might notice something out of one eye, such as a mailbox, and as he continues along, his other eye may then catch sight of the mailbox. Because of the distance between his eyes, and particularly because he did not change his vision and use both eyes to focus on it, the mailbox will appear to move from one side to the other. This, combined with the horse's tendency to leave first and investigate later, may cause him to shy at the mailbox.

■ *The horse processes different information with each eye. Just because he is comfortable in the round pen traveling to the left (watching you with his left eye) doesn't mean he will be as comfortable watching you out of his right eye. In fact, you'll find him trying to put you on one side or the other. Horses are particularly sensitive to objects that have moved. A horse may have seen a garbage can on the left of the barn door every day, but if you move it to the right, it's as if he's never seen it before. In reality, he hasn't seen it with that eye.*

The horse's eyes and ears work as a team.

In mounted work, when you swing your right leg over your horse's back, it will suddenly appear in the field of vision of his right eye. He may also be able to see your hands on the reins depending on the position of his head. If you swing the end of the reins or a whip toward his head, he may react. This is why it is so important to be sure that you have thoroughly sacked him out. If a horse is head-shy, there's a good chance he's going to buck when he's ridden and gets startled by something near his ears.

■ *The horse has a blind spot directly behind his head. If his head is held straight ahead of him and level with his body, he can't see behind his hindquarters. If he is unaware of your presence, and you approach in this blind spot, you may startle him. This is why you should always speak to be sure the horse knows you are there, and watch to see him turn his head and look, before you approach his hindquarters.*

■ *While one eye will allow the horse to detect movement, he needs both eyes to judge distance, width, depth or height. This is called "binocular vision" and is in use when both ears are pricked forward. A horse uses binocular vision to navigate a creek or jump. Too-abrupt or poorly timed rein movements can cause the horse to raise his head as he approaches, which can keep him from focusing on the obstacle and can result in awkward strides. If the rider slows or gathers the horse smoothly and well ahead of the obstacle, the horse's visual abilities are maximized.*

When using binocular vision, the horse focuses on far objects by raising his nose in relation to his head. Watch a horse as he looks for his pasturemates across a field. Conversely, lowering his nose brings closer objects into focus. Riding toward a pole on the ground in the arena, you'll find the horse lowering his head and bringing his nose in to focus on it. If we want the horse to be able to see where he's going, we must allow him some freedom of of his head when riding. Too high, and he can't see the ground. Too low and he can't see ahead.

■ *The horse cannot see under his nose. So for instance, when his head is out front and he's walking down the trail, he cannot see his front feet hit the ground. Conveniently, that's not any more necessary for him than it is for us. He doesn't need to see his hind feet set down, either, to be surefooted. If you watch a horse walk on a rocky or uneven trail, you'll see him put his find feet down close to where the front feet just left, which allows him predictable footing.*

■ *Horses' pupils are horizontal because prey animals need to see as widely as possible around themselves to avoid predators. Contrast this with cats, who are predators and have vertical pupils. Given horizontal pupils, his vision above head height is not particularly good.*

■ *At the top edge of the horse's pupil (within his eyeball), projecting horizontally outward from the iris, are dark, finger-like projections. These "corpora nigra" act as sun shades for the pupil.*

> ■ *Older horses, and thin ones, have depressions above
> their eye sockets that are normally filled with fatty tissue.
> Horses tend to lose the fat deposit here as they get older,
> even if they carry good body weight. If the eye gets hit,
> the eyeball presses against this fatty pad, which rises and
> makes room for it, preventing damage to the eyeball.*

Ya gotta have a friend

The wild-horse social system involves bands of mares and their
offspring. The lead mare takes others to food, water and safety.
The stallion looks out for other stallions who may steal his mares,
keeps a close eye on his band so none stray, keeps them rounded
up together for safety, and follows his band to food and water. As
colts mature and threaten the stallion's leadership, they are chased
off to form bachelor bands.

For horses, there is safety in numbers. Young horses keep close
to their dams, and the band members keep close to each other. The
distance narrows in threatening times and widens as it's safe. If it's
safe enough for the lead mare to stop and urinate, you'll find the

Horses believe there is safety in numbers.

other band members doing so also. If one or more of the band bolts, the others will follow, even though they might not have identified the threat.

For this reason, riding in a pasture with loose horses may get you in trouble. If they take off running, your horse will have a strong instinct to follow. When riding with another rider, running your horse up to or past his horse may cause his horse to startle and run also.

This instinctive desire to stay together is manifested in alertness, whinnying, nervousness or even berserk behavior in one or both horses when they are separated. If you and a friend trailer your horses to a show together, even if the horses have never lived together, you might find them whinnying for each other when one is tied at the trailer and the other is taken into the warm-up area.

The better trained the horse, the more he will look to his rider for direction and the less dependent he will be on the herd instinct or activity of other horses. While convenience dictates that any horse should calmly allow himself to be ridden away from the herd or be left behind by the herd, this is not always so. When trail riding, the others should wait while one rider remounts, for example, after opening a gate or adjusting his tack. If the group was to ride away — particularly quickly or disappear from sight — it may make it difficult or dangerous for the rider left behind to mount and catch up in a controlled manner.

Wild horses compete for resources such as food and water. The dominant or stronger animals get to eat or drink or run down the path first. These relationships are quite complex. Members are constantly interacting, and many closely ranked animals threaten each other often. Either horse may initiate the interaction, but the dominant one is the one who refuses to give ground, while the submissive one ceases to challenge or moves away.

You may have seen the submissive mouthing or chewing behavior of a foal in the presence of any adult other than his mother. **Submissive behaviors like this keep conflict from occurring and keep horses from getting hurt in more active altercations.** Be aware that approaching a horse while he is eating might elicit a defensive behavior.

While you are probably comfortable when your parent or spouse stands close to you, you expect someone you know less well to stay farther away. Horses feel similarly. If you watch horses interacting, you will see differences in personal space between different horses. Problems and accidents may occur when handlers are unaware of the horses' social interactions.

John is using the "first get the feet to move" rule, just as a dominant horse in the herd would.

Home equals safety and comfort

Home is a safe, comfortable place. When you take the horse out to the round pen, arena or trail, it will be clear that he knows where home is. In the arena, he will slow or stop on the barn side of the arena, or attempt to leave if the gate is open. Be careful that you don't encourage balking at the gate by allowing him to stop there. Don't run him toward the gate and stop too many times, or you'll find it difficult to get him back toward the far end of the arena. The same holds true for the trail. Horses have excellent homing senses and will know immediately when you've turned around to head home. If you let him go too fast or get out of control running toward home you've encouraged his natural urge to go toward his place of comfort. ■

3

Solving Pasture Problems

Keeping your horses all one happy family takes more than good intentions — it takes careful consideration of the relationships in the group, and it takes knowing how to deal with each personality.

L ast chapter, we talked about the intricacies of social interactions between horses on pasture and how to properly introduce a new horse to the group. In this chapter, we will look at more equine behaviors and commonly encountered problems, and we'll give you some basic advice on keeping horses at pasture happy and healthy.

The bully

A bully (or bully-ette) — usually a gelding with stallion characteristics or an alpha/aggressive mare — can disrupt the peace on pasture. But, if he/she is not posing a serious physical threat to the rest of the group, you may decide to pasture her anyway and work to decrease the number of situations likely to trigger aggressive behavior.

The neighborhood bully is most likely to show aggression around grain-feeding time. Make sure you have an adequate arrangement for feeding in the field and plan on feeding the bully first — a decision that is likely to be made for you anyway!

It helps to place the bully's feed tub at a generous distance (at least two to three horse lengths) away from the other horses. Whenever possible, have someone help you at feeding time. One of you should feed the bully while the other takes care of the remaining horses. **If your bully refuses to settle for his own feed tub and insists on making**

Historically, it was thought that a natural water source was best. Using a pond or stream as the primary water source for horses, however, leads to erosion problems. Also, you cannot monitor the quality of the water.

the rounds of everyone else's bucket for the entire feeding time, you may have to consider feeding him separately. Alternatively, if the horse is safe to tie, keep a tie rope beside the feed tub and keep the bully tied until everyone else has finished.

When feeding hay, you may have to break the rule against feeding on the ground if your group has a bully. Often, an effective strategy is to place more piles of hay than there are horses, and space the piles a generous distance from each other (outside kicking range between horses). Hay takes longer to eat, so there is not as much danger of the bully getting too much of another horse's share. There is likely to be a period of "musical piles" as the bully chases a few horses away from their hay, but this should settle down within a few minutes. The bully will quickly realize he is spending more time chasing than eating.

Another high-risk time for aggression is when the horses are being brought in from the field (assuming they want to come in). The bully will usually insist on coming in first. Your wisest move is to do exactly that. Put a lead rope on your problem horse and remove him from the group as quickly as possible, leaving little time for biting, charging or kicking the others.

With an exceptionally aggressive horse, it is important to make sure you have the horse's attention before going into the field to catch him. A horse who is busy chasing, charging or attacking other horses could easily catch you in the crossfire, or you could be injured when the intended "victim" tries to get out of range.

Do not attempt to break up any confrontations when the horses are loose. You will not have adequate control, and you should NEVER start any interaction with an aggressive horse that you cannot finish with the horse under control. Once the horse has been caught and the lead rope is in place, insist on obedience and socially acceptable behavior. His/her reward will be prompt removal from the field ahead of everyone else.

It is usually not a good idea to try to teach the horse a lesson by holding him back and allowing the other horses to be removed from the field first. Not only will the horse be extremely difficult to manage during this time, but you will cause him to "lose face" with the group, potentially leading to even more aggression to reestablish who is No. 1 the next time the situation arises.

Remember, too, that there is nothing you can do to "train" the horse to behave when he is loose in the pasture. Your influence disappears with your physical presence. Peace and order will be established more quickly if you do not interfere with herd politics. Instead, allow the horses to establish for themselves where they stand in the social order. When interacting with the horse one-to-one at the end of the lead rope, however, you should insist on 100 percent obedience. The horse should never get away with threatening looks/ear pinning, kicking, etc. when you are leading him.

The kicker

Another real headache in a group of horses is the animal who kicks at the others with the slightest provocation. This may occur when another horse approaches either too closely or from an unacceptable direction (usually the rear or flank). This behavior is the hallmark of an irritable mare but is certainly not unheard of in geldings. Or it may only be evident when the horses are running around or otherwise at play — more an outbreak of exuberance than malice. Regardless of the individual's personality or intentions, there is again virtually nothing you can do to control this behavior when the horses are loose in the field. Rest assured, however, the members of the group will quickly come to recognize the horse who has a propensity to kick and will steer clear.

The kicker will pose particular problems under the same circumstances as the bully — feeding time and when being brought out of the field. The same common-sense measures used for the bully should be used with the kicker (adequate distance between feeding locations, bring the kicker out of the group quickly, and so forth). **You should also be careful never to herd a group of horses containing a kicker (or a bully) into a small area.** Kickers should never be turned out in a group when they have back shoes on. The sheer force of a kick is bad enough. If the horse is wearing shoes, it is like arming him with brass knuckles, as well.

The outcast

Within a band of horses, you will frequently notice several small divisions of two or more who "hang out" together, grazing in the same locations, playing with each other, etc. In groups of horses of three or more, there is likely to be at least one animal who is on the fringes and is lowest in social status. This horse will be the last to

In some circumstances, feeding on the ground like this is acceptable. However, the use of feed bunkers is preferable. Be sure to put hay piles far enough apart that each horse can eat without feeling threatened.

eat, drink and be brought in from the field. The newest member of a group, unless he is more aggressive than the average horse, will have this position at least temporarily, until he is accepted into one of the smaller groups. The assimilation process usually occurs smoothly and within a matter of days.

Problems are more likely to occur when the band is small and all members are closely attached, or if the new horse has a physical problem that makes him an easy target for intimidation. **Even horses who have been within a group for a considerable time may lose their social standing and become outcasts if they develop a physical problem that makes them obviously unable to compete with the others for food, water or choice grazing locations.** When a horse who had previously been well-incorporated into the group becomes an outcast, it is important to look for a cause. Isolation often means that the horse is ill, injured or lame and needs your attention.

THERE IS NOTHING YOU CAN DO TO "TRAIN" THE HORSE TO BEHAVE WHEN HE IS LOOSE IN THE PASTURE.

As long as the outcast is not being physically hurt by the other horses, it is safe to leave him with the group if adequate measures are taken to ensure the horse gets enough to eat. Newcomers who have trouble finding their niche may benefit from spending a few days in a smaller paddock with one of the least aggressive horses from the band; these two may form enough of a bond during that time that the newcomer can be reintroduced to the band with a friend at his/her side.

It is interesting to note that horses who are obviously meek and submissive in the herd may be aggressive and difficult to handle by people. They may also become bullies if removed from the original situation and put in a small group with horses they can easily intimidate. While it is not appropriate to describe equine behavior in human terms, it appears these horses store up quite a bit of frustration and unleash it when they find themselves in a situation where they can be the physically superior participant.

The fence (or tree) chewer

A less complicated but extremely annoying behavior of horses at pasture is chewing fences or trees. In most cases, this occurs because of insufficient grass or hay. A horse's strongest drive, and the activity that keeps his attention for the greatest part of the day, is eating. Because a horse's natural diet takes a long time to digest, he is programmed to graze continuously. When there is nothing else left to graze, the horse turns to fencing or trees. **The most effective cure is to avoid overgrazing or make sure there is always a generous supply of hay.**

You can stretch your hay dollar by buying grass hays that were cut after the blooming stage. Horses will even happily munch at straw if nothing else is available. (Seek expert advice regarding needed supplements of protein, minerals and vitamins if you feed late-maturity hays to keep the horses occupied.) No hays with mold or excessive dirt should ever be used.

If providing more hay does not solve the problem, or if you have a horse who seems determined to destroy fencing and trees regardless of how much hay is available, other measures will be needed. Painting the fencing with bitter-tasting substances is one approach that works, but this has to be done repeatedly and in the end is not cost-effective or time-efficient.

The best approach in most circumstances is to install a "hot wire," an electrified wire to keep horses away from the fencing. Hot wires are most efficient when they project several inches from the wood.

Trees can be protected to some extent by placing cages around them. Wire works well for this but is a bit of a safety risk, as horses seem to have a real talent for managing to become injured or entangled in any wire in their vicinity. Constructing a small fence around trees using the newer plastic fencing materials may be a safer and more attractive alternative than wire.

Quick check

Minor illnesses, injuries or lamenesses are easy to miss in horses at pasture but can quickly turn into more serious problems if unattended. If you make it a habit to be observant whenever you are around the horses, you will be less likely to overlook early signs of problems. Feeding and watering time is best for checking the herd.

As you approach, check to see if any of the horses are standing off by themselves or are slow to come to eat or drink. **Isolation is often the first sign that something is wrong.** *Watch the horses for any signs of lameness. After they have settled down to eat, make a quick visual check of each animal for discharge from the eyes or nose, bleeding, cuts, unusual swellings, staining from diarrhea, etc. Note any coughing when eating or drinking. If the group is small and well-mannered when eating, you might also want to go into the field and quickly run your hands down each leg and over the surface of the foot, checking for heat or swelling. Also make a close-up check of the horse's entire body, including the undersurface of the belly and sheath in geldings or stallions. These few extra minutes of attention will pay off in early detection and treatment of injuries or sickness.*

Feeding hay in the field

The greatest challenge in feeding horses at pasture is to ensure each horse has an equal chance to eat. Second to that is keeping waste to a minimum. Ideally, horses should be fed from bunkers or hay racks rather than on the ground. Ground feeding increases exposure to parasites and is also wasteful, as a considerable percentage of the hay will be trampled.

For large groups, racks built into the walls of a sizable shed are the most practical arrangement. The shed should be large enough that all horses fit inside, with sufficient room between to keep them out of kicking range of their neighbor. Sheds also provide protection from the elements for both the horses and your hay.

Next best is the use of bunkers. How many bunkers are needed will be determined by how many horses there are and how well they get along. Ideally each horse will be out of range of his neighbor's kick, but in large groups this is rarely practical. Try to provide a minimum of three to five feet between horses around the bunker to allow some maneuverability.

If a shed or feed bunkers are not options, hay will have to be fed from the ground. When doing this, choose a location away from muddy, high-traffic areas. Set out the hay in individual piles (enough for one horse) and allow for generous spacing (10 feet or so) between piles. In large groups, there is inevitably going to be competition and one or more horses who will insist on checking out each of the piles to guarantee they get the choicest hay (see bullies, above). To guarantee each horse gets hay, set out at least one extra pile.

Human safety is always a consideration at feeding time, especially in a large group. The best way to distribute hay piles or fill bunkers/racks is from the bed of a pick-up or from a wagon. The horses may not be deliberately trying to hurt you, but the center of a group of hungry horses is no place to be on foot. You can be jostled, knocked about, stepped on or worse in the initial flurry of activity and competition.

Feeding grain in the field

Grain feeding under pasture conditions can be more of a challenge than working out a system for haying. Grain cannot be fed from the ground and must be placed in a solid container that will not spill. Deep troughs work best for avoiding waste, but horses will be even more competitive about getting grain than getting hay, and fighting at bunkers is a big problem.

Again, the best arrangement is a generous-sized shed with a trough running the entire length of the sides and enough room for horses to position themselves outside of kicking range. Bunkers will work, too, but you need to be more generous in the room available between horses.

In many ways, individual buckets are best. There is less chance of stronger horses bolting their feed and stealing that of the weaker ones. You can make sure that individual portions are the size you want them to be. Buckets secured along the fence line can be filled without entering the field and risking injury. They are also easier to keep clean than a trough or large feeder.

Buckets must be secured to the fence in such a way that they cannot be tipped or spilled by the horses. Brackets are ideal, but even tight bungie cords around the middle of the buckets to hold the buckets snuggly will work.

We recommend you use either deep buckets or buckets with inside rims to minimize loss of grain from horses who like to throw it around or dig through it when eating. Be generous in the spacing between buckets — i.e., out of kicking range of the neighbor. Finally, always put out one more bucket of grain than the number of horses in the field. The propensity of horses to check out their neighbor's feed is great, and you want to make sure every horse gets a chance to eat.

Salt

Don't forget that all horses need constant access to salt. All hay-and-grain diets are deficient in this important element. Large blocks are available for field use and should be placed in a sheltered location, preferably in a shed or bunker where the horses eat.

Watering arrangements

Natural water sources such as streams or ponds can effectively meet the horses' needs and are certainly the most attractive in terms of saving time and labor. However, these may be a prime location for picking up EPM organisms, as all the neighborhood wildlife will use them, too. Automatic waterers are available for convenient outdoor use, but they're often difficult to keep clean. Watering from buckets is fine if you don't mind constantly refilling them (horses should never run out of water).

The best compromise in terms of optimal use of your time, keeping an adequate supply available and easy cleaning is often to use either a bathtub or plastic/metal livestock watering tub. The bathtub has the advantage of draining from the bottom for easy cleaning, but the livestock tubs are fairly lightweight when empty.

Whatever arrangement you use, water buckets or tubs should be cleaned out with a brush on a daily basis, using cleanser (Ajax, Comet, etc.) if needed to remove dirt, scum and algae from the sides. Cleanser rinses off easier than soaps or detergents, and if adequately rinsed off will not leave an unpleasant residue that could inhibit drinking. ▣

A retired bathtub can make a great waterer — easy to clean and to drain. But make sure you don't use one like this, with sharp edges that a horse could run into or get cut on.

Notes

4

Making Introductions

*A new horse entering a herd can have a harder day
than a new kid at school. So when you
bring home a new horse, what can you do
to help him make friends?*

It sounds so appealing... Just put up a good fence around that plot of grass behind your house, add a few horses, then sit back on the porch with your feet propped up and enjoy the idyllic scene. Unfortunately, by choosing horses as the critters to liven up your landscape, you will quickly find that the instinctive behavior patterns of the wild horse are still very much in operation in the domesticated horse, which can cause you some real headaches. Here's how to help your horses get along with each other, so you can get back to that porch and enjoy the view!

The role of stallion

When you look out at a group of horses quietly grazing, you might guess there is a complex social structure, a hierarchy or "pecking order" that maintains the peace. The band bears more resemblance to a disciplined army unit than a social club.

In the wild, the band is overseen by a single stallion. The only other males tolerated are young foals and juveniles who have not reached sexual maturity (usually well under the age of two). As males are weaned, they are rejected by their dams. When they begin to show signs of maturity, the stallion will drive them from the herd. Young male stallions wander the range alone in search of mares to build their own band.

A new horse has to quickly determine his place in the herd. A threat not heeded becomes a physical attack.

The stallion's primary duty is that of lookout. He is constantly on the alert for danger, posed by either predators or other stallions seeking to disrupt the group and steal mares. In times of danger, he will scream the alert that will unify and mobilize the band. **The stallion has little to do with the routine, day-to-day interactions between the mares, though.** The social structure within the band is female-dominated, and it is these relationships that are of greatest interest to us.

The role of the mare

The stallion is king, and he most definitely has a queen. The queen is known as the "alpha mare." **It is the alpha mare who makes such decisions as when the group will move on to look for better grazing or water.** The alpha mare rules with complete and utter authority. Any mare who oversteps her bounds, does not comply with directions to move on, or attempts to infringe on the rights of another mare (i.e., to a choice grazing spot) is dealt with quickly and harshly with a bite, kick or strike. The other mares in the band have rank and privileges that are determined partially by their time within the band and partially by their size, strength and aggressiveness. The stronger, more aggressive mares have a higher standing. Mares of similar social class will tend to cluster together in small groups. Newcomers and weaker horses frequent the fringes of the group, either alone or in pairs (misery loves company).

A mare can advance her social standing by taking the place of a higher-ranking mare who dies or is left behind because she is injured, or by directly challenging a higher-ranking mare for the rights to one of her privileges. Any mare who wishes to advance her standing must be prepared for a show of physical strength and aggression. A fight between mares is no laughing matter. They will square off and bite, kick and strike as viciously as any pair of stallions.

Back at the farm

The social interactions in your backyard are somewhat different but have many similarities to natural band behavior. **Just like in the wild, most problems with fighting, bickering and aggression will involve a mare.** Mares are more inclined to physical (unfriendly) contact than many geldings. They will fight either with other mares or with geldings. If you happen to have a mare with an alpha-mare personality in your group, you will have real headaches. These mares are constantly bothering other horses, nipping or kicking at them, essentially bullying them around and giving orders.

A mare of this type is especially dangerous when it comes time to bring horses in from the field or to feed. When she gets in close quarters, she can do some real damage.

Fortunately, few mares will display this degree of aggression. **However, as a general rule, a mare is more likely than a gelding to actually bite, strike or kick another horse.** Mares also do a lot more squealing and yelling than geldings. **Vocalizing is a prelude to aggression and a warning that the other horse has not been accepted in her "personal space."** It is often accompanied by foot-stomping, half-rearing or other intimidating movements, and may directly precede an actual blow or bite. In other words, **squeals are not idle threats**! There are also many mares who are extremely docile and passive in a group, yet who, ironically, can sometimes be the ones with the most training problems or who will become aggressive if moved to a different social situation — almost as if they are releasing their built-up frustrations.

Geldings will vary widely in how they behave in a group. Some retain obvious stallion characteristics: keeping largely to themselves, appearing vigilant and more active than the other horses, even fighting with other geldings or attempting to breed mares. Actual fights between geldings, however, will usually not occur unless there is another one in the group with the same behavior characteristics. And the gelding who behaves like a stallion will never fight with a mare or even defend himself against a mare. (Chivalry is very much alive among horses.) For the most part, geldings are rather easygoing and blend well into groups of horses. The most dangerous period in terms of horses hurting each other will be when a new one is introduced into the group.

Introducing new horses to the group

It is never a good idea to put a strange horse out with a group — or, for that matter, to turn an unfamiliar horse out with even a single horse. **Horses crave the companionship of other horses, but they also have a ritual for sizing each other up and deciding if the stranger can be accepted or should be challenged.**

When you get a new horse, do not force any introductions. Lead the newcomer around in front of the others while they are in their stalls or in a paddock/field but where they cannot get direct contact. Do not let the horses directly face each other, even if they are obviously interested. Let the idea of a new horse sink in for a few days first. If you know you have a leader or more aggressive horse in your group, this is the one you need to win over. If he accepts the new horse, the others more than likely will also.

To begin introductions, allow the horses to extend their necks until they can touch noses. The loose horse should be inside a stall or on the other side of a gate where he cannot get a leg caught if striking. Keep the newcomer on a lead shank and allow him no closer than needed just to allow noses to touch. Do not position yourself between the horses or in front of their legs because of the danger of sudden bites or strikes. Stand at the newcomer's shoulder, allowing plenty of room to pull him back or to circle out of range of the other horse. **Allow only a few sniffs the first time, then break it off, walking the newcomer away.** This mimics what would happen if there was immediate acceptance — they would sniff briefly, then go about their own business.

After a few minutes, bring the horse back again for nose contact. This time, allow them to touch noses and sniff without interruption unless squealing, foot-stomping or striking occurs. If they (or one) squeal, break off contact, walk the newcomer away and try again later. Once signs of aggression have stopped or at least are restricted to a token, much toned-down squeal or stomp, allow the horses to

Allow the horses to extend their necks until they can just touch noses, but be sure you are standing in a location where you cannot get hurt should one of them make a sudden move.

get a little closer, to the point they can just reach the other horse's neck. Again, always keep yourself out of harm's way — back at the shoulder and in a spot where you have plenty of room to maneuver both yourself and the horse. They will likely arch their necks at this point, keeping their noses in close contact as they continue to sniff and blow at each other.

When the nose contact breaks off, they will work their way slowly down each other's necks, sniffing gently. Squeals, stomps or strikes can occur at any time in this process if one of the horses decides the other is taking too much liberty with entering his personal space. If the objection is mild, prevent the newcomer from moving any farther down the other's neck, but allow sniffing to continue. If the threats seem more obvious or one tries to bite, break it off. Better safe than sorry. Walk away and try again later, after both have cooled off.

Continue the introduction process by letting the horses get to the point where they have sniffed down as far as each other's shoulders with no serious signs of aggression (no actual biting or striking). A few squeals or stomps are almost inevitable once the horses are actually making body contact for the first time. You can allow that, but you must be ready to break it off for biting or striking. **Once they mutually tolerate the sniffing as far back as the shoulder, you have crossed a major hurdle.**

The next step is to allow full-body sniffing (this is what they will do when you finally put them out in the field together). To begin this process under conditions where you still have some control, turn the newcomer so that his body is just within reach of the other horse's nose. Stand more to the front of the horse for this, as he may try to swing away from the sniffing, and don't get between the two horses. If all goes well, the newcomer will be sniffed from head to tail without showing any more resistance than some flicking of the skin or a little tail swishing. Your other horse will finish the sniffing and, if the horse is accepted, will quickly lose interest and walk away to find something better to do. **As with the other introductory steps, striking, biting or kicking attempts are your signal to cut it off, walk the horse away and try again after both horses have calmed down.**

This same introductory sequence should be followed with each horse in the group before you turn the newcomer loose in the band. You will find that in many cases, it is accomplished quickly and easily — in less time than it just took you to read about it. If you have gotten all the horses through their introductions without a serious incident, it is time to put the newcomer in the field with the group. It is helpful to have someone there to assist, keeping the other horses away from the gate and from the new horse long enough for you to get him to a spot where he will not be easily forced into a corner and feel threatened. **Make sure the horse is facing you when you turn him loose. Then, quickly get out of range.** Excited horses are more prone to buck and kick when turned loose.

It is a good idea to remove the other horses from the pasture and let the newcomer explore it on his own for a few hours before letting the horses loose together. This allows him to get a feel for the "lay of the land" and become somewhat familiar with his boundaries so he is less likely to get cornered or injured on fencing, wire, etc., which he might not notice in the event one of the group becomes aggressive. While the horse is investigating his new surroundings, it is also a good idea for you to carefully check for damage to fencing, buildings, feeders, etc., and correct any weaknesses or dangerous areas such as sharp projections that could injure a horse whose attention is focused elsewhere.

You will probably find that, once loose together, one or more of the horses will repeat the sniffing/body contact sequence again, perhaps even with some squealing or a few minor scuffles for a day or so as ground rules get established. This is unavoidable, but if you've done your introductions well, there will a minimum of fuss and much less risk of a serious bite, strike or kick.

Breaking up fights

Serious fighting between horses in a group is rare. **In fact, one of the major purposes of the complicated social structure in a band of horses is to assign every horse a "place" or "rank" to prevent fighting.** Disputes are usually quickly settled by a clear show of intent (ear-pinning, teeth-baring, charging, etc.) on the part of the dominant horse, with no need for actual physical contact. A major source of actual fighting is the appearance of a new horse, which is why we urge you to take the time to make gradual introductions before putting the horse out with the group.

If a serious fight does break out, do NOT jump the fence and rush into the middle of it. If threat of harm by another horse is not causing one of them to back down, you will most certainly not intimidate them and you could easily get hurt. From a safe distance, try loud and angry yelling or a loud whip crack and a few well-placed rock throws (to get their attention — not to hit them) to break their focus on each other, allowing one or both to decide they've had enough. If you persevere, this will work. Do not approach either horse until you're sure you have his attention. Horses become agitated and focused in a fight. Their eyes have a characteristic glazed-over appearance that will gradually disappear and soften as they

Even after the introductions are made successfully, there may be a few days of mild turmoil as relationships are established.

calm down. Approaching them before they "come back to earth" is dangerous.

If there are no injuries that require attention, it is best to leave them both where they are, to think about what happened and hopefully at least come to a mutual non-aggression pact. **If two horses repeatedly have serious fights, you will have to accept the fact that both are aggressive and evenly matched (fighting would stop if there was a clear winner). Different turnout arrangements will be needed if you want to keep both horses.**

Born enemies

You may occasionally find two horses who seem to absolutely hate each other and who resist all attempts at peaceful introduction. This is more likely to happen between two geldings than two mares. Mares will often require a longer and more gradual introduction period but seem to be better able to eventually get things straightened out than two geldings who dislike each other.

You may be able to tone down the aggression by constant exposure at a safe distance. Tie the new horse where the other can see and smell him but not reach him. Walk him past the other horse frequently, but always keep well out of range. When they seem to at least accept the other's nearby presence without showing any aggression, allow some tentative and very brief nose-to-nose contact, never allowing them enough contact to get worked up. If they can be convinced to tolerate each other to this degree, there is a better chance you can successfully put them out in a group together without a serious fight. They will simply stay away from each other.

It will also help if you can identify a horse within the group who accepts the newcomer well and is not one of the close "buddies" of the aggressor. This will probably be one of the horses at the bottom of the pecking order (last to come in, etc.). Allow the newcomer and the accepting horse a few days alone in a paddock together. The newcomer will now automatically have a "place" in the group by association with the other horse. You can then try putting the pair in with the larger group.

The extremely aggressive horse

Dear Perfect Horse,

My first horse purchase was a package deal: a Quarter Horse mare and a small Arab gelding who had been together for five years. He appeared to be a real sweetheart until several months later when I bought a young Belgian gelding. The new horse was in an adjacent enclosure. He was fine with the mare, but the Arab gelding would lunge and bite at the Belgian over the fence. After months of separation, the Arab went through the fence, terrorized the Belgian, who tried to run away and ended up a bloody mess. Please tell me how to remedy the problem.

The heart of your problem may be the adage, "Two's company, three's a crowd." In essence, your pre-Belgian arrangement was like that of a one-mare, one-stallion band. Some geldings retain many of the physical and personality traits of a stallion, even to the point of mounting mares.

Your Arabian's aggression is most reminiscent of a stallion fighting to keep a mare from being stolen. His degree of aggression, however, goes several steps beyond what might be expected, even in a real-life situation involving actual stallions. Something else is going on here, as well.

You didn't mention the relative sizes of the horses, but even a young horse of a draft breed will probably be more physically imposing than an Arab. Your Arabian may be trying to intimidate the newcomer by a greater show of aggression.

What doesn't fit with normal behavior patterns is his apparent determination to do bodily harm. Stallions on breeding farms are often turned out in adjacent paddocks separated only by a walkway to prevent direct contact but in full view of each other, yet they don't crash through fencing to pick fights. You also didn't mention how the young horse reacts to this, but it's a good bet that even if *he is bigger, the behavior of the older horse scares him to death. A young horse rarely has enough self-confidence to stand up to threats from a mature animal. If he's acting nonchalant, however, that may be the trigger that pushed the Arab over the edge and made him determined to "get" the newcomer.*

If your young horse is obviously frightened, and the older one is pursuing him anyway, this behavior is not normal. The Arabian may have been in a bad social situation where he was "low man" and harassed by bigger or stronger horses before you purchased him. Such horses will often become terrible bullies themselves if moved to a new situation where they can be the "top dog."

So, what can you do about it? Nothing you do will change the personality of the Arab, and there are no training methods that will carry over to how he behaves on pasture when you are not around to intervene. One solution, although seemingly extreme, may be to return the Belgian to his former owners and replace him with a mare. Your Arabian should react differently to a mare — although we must warn you that the other mare could then become an aggressor, depending on her personality!

Another possibility is to temporarily remove your mare from the equation. Try to find someone who will keep her for you for a few weeks. After a few days, the Arabian should realize she is gone and calm down. At that time, gradually begin reintroducing the other two. Horses are extremely social animals and crave companionship. The first positive sign would be a reduction in the Arab's degree of aggression (i.e., not charging at the newcomer, no teeth baring, etc.). Once this occurs, you can again try putting them in adjacent paddocks and eventually in a paddock together. Only if and when they have successfully formed a bond should you try to bring the mare back — and NOT at a time when she is in season! Follow the same steps for introducing the mare back to each of the other two horses. Hopefully the result will be one big happy family — or at least a level of acceptance that prevents any of them from being hurt. **PH**

5

Living With Stallions

*As children, most of us grew up with
a fascination for stallions. We read the
"Black Stallion" books by Walter Farley, so it's logical
that our stallion will be just like that. Right?*

We watched Roy Rogers and Trigger fight bad guys in the old West. We watched in awe as the white stallions of the Spanish Riding School performed airs above the ground. Today, we see John and Bright Zip working together as two halves of a whole. As a result, we romanticize the image of the stallion, and many of us dream of owning one. But before you make the decision to buy a stallion, or to leave that young colt ungelded, you need to understand the reality of day-to-day life with a stallion.

Characteristics of stallions

To understand stallions, it is helpful to examine how horses live and behave in the wild. Colts are born into a herd environment where many mares live in a band, protected by one mature stallion. Later, during their early years, the bachelor colts will band together. As they mature, the young stallions will leave the bachelor bands to build herds of their own. In order to do that, they must battle with other stallions to steal mares from an existing band. Once a stallion establishes his own herd, he breeds all the mares in it and protects the band from other stallions.

This lifestyle pattern tells us that stallions are put on this earth to perform two functions — to breed and to fight. Neither of these

This stallion can enjoy the company of another horse without risk of injury — they are separated by two fences and a 12-foot lane.

characteristics, however, is desirable in a performance horse. When working with stallions, the challenge is to control the stallion's natural responses and to redirect his energies into more productive activities. **We must motivate the stallion to perform without invoking his instinct to fight.** The failure to understand this balance has led to myriad sad stories about vicious stallions and incredibly cruel training practices used to control their natural behavior.

Another observation can be made from the natural, wild-horse lifestyle pattern. Young stallions are submissive to the other horses at the time they are driven from the herd. As young bachelors, they play hard among themselves. As they grow stronger and older, they begin to challenge other horses for social standing. Many people do not understand this and are surprised when their six-year-old stallion is suddenly hard to control, when previously he was always sweet and biddable. **The fact is that stallions become progressively more aggressive as they get older. Don't be fooled into leaving that colt ungelded just because he is a sweet two-year-old. Only solid, consistent training will maintain that sweetness into the horse's old age.**

One of the most important factors when dealing with stallions is that they require a great deal of attention, much more than geldings or mares, and lots of physical contact. They need mental stimulation to reduce the boredom of stable life. Stallions generally have a higher energy level and therefore will be quicker to develop bad habits when bored.

Stallion ownership is not for the weekend warrior. A stallion kept in a standard stable arrangement must be ridden or handled at least five days a week. These interactions can be performance-training sessions, trail rides, ground-training sessions or just extended grooming times on days when it is too nasty to go outside. **Consistent, daily interaction with a stallion will go a long way to avoiding future behavior problems.**

Interacting with stallions

A stallion must understand that humans are above him in the social order. The people who have the best relationships with their stallions have established that fact in the horse's mind using a combination of firmness and affection. The problem with "showing him who's boss" using brute force, aside from the obvious humane reason, is that it's very difficult to challenge a stallion and win. As soon as you challenge him in a belligerent manner, you activate his instinct to fight. Once a stallion decides to fight, you are in danger. He has a battery of defenses, including biting, striking, rearing and charging, any of which can seriously injure you or others.

The safest and most effective way to establish dominance over a stallion is to do so in small increments, repeated thousands of times. For instance, every time he is asked to move over on the wash rack, to move his feet so his stall can be cleaned or to drop his head so he can be bridled, he has been asked to accept a human as his social superior.

The opposite is also true. **Every time the horse moves toward you and you move away, you have reinforced to him that he is higher than you in the social order.** This is a dangerous precedent. The stallion must not be allowed to move you around. This is where attention to body language and small details is important. When you walk into him, he should move out of the way. He should not try to move into you at any time, with any part of his body. Many people ignore these small things and are later surprised when their stallion suddenly charges past them out of a stall, pins them against the wall in the wash rack or becomes a complete bully when being led.

There is another important difference in dealing with stallions, as opposed to mares or geldings — **stallions have a rigid sense of** justice. **They make a distinction between what they consider to be discipline and what they consider to be abuse.** A stallion will accept discipline, but he will fight you if you cross into his definition of abuse. Sometimes, a stallion will tolerate a chain for a time and then decide he's had enough. The next person to put the chain on him may be seriously injured when the stallion reacts to what he considers abuse. Each horse has a different tolerance level. When training a stallion, it's important to watch his body language to know how far to extend a training session and when to take a break.

In an attempt to control their stallion's behavior, people have resorted to a variety of devices, all of which have one thing in common — they cause the horse pain. Many stallions are forced to endure chains over their noses, under their chins and over their lips. When pulled, the chains cause the horse pain by putting pressure on sensitive tissues.

The use of pain to control a horse becomes less effective over time. In order to maintain the same level of control, the pain must be increased. As the pain level is increased, the horse's determination to fight it increases. This is ultimately a no-win, dangerous situation.

The use of pain also encourages undesirable behavior. For instance, pulling down on a stud chain will usually cause a horse to raise his head. If he raises it high enough, his front feet will also come off the ground. Once he rears, the stallion may strike at the handler or use the leverage he gains to pull free and run away.

Evaluating a stallion prospect

In addition to the many aspects of owning and housing a stallion, you should objectively evaluate your colt's potential as a sire. He should be an outstanding example of his breed, with strong breed characteristics and a sound temperament. If his breed registration is based upon bloodlines, such as with Quarter Horses, Thoroughbreds and Tennessee Walking Horses, it is preferable that he be descended from bloodlines that are known for their good temperament and athletic ability. In breeds that require certification or approval of breeding stallions, such as many warmblood registries, the stallion prospect should have a high approval rating or be capable of earning such a rating. For color-based breeds, consider your prospect's genetic chance of producing the desired color.

Mare owners will consider all these factors when selecting a stallion. Do not overestimate the number of mares your stallion will breed each year. The fact is that stallions are plentiful in almost all breeds, and he is unlikely to breed more than a few outside mares a year, unless your horse has a national show record or an outstanding pedigree.

THERE IS NO REASON WHY A PROPERLY TRAINED STALLION CAN'T BE UNDER CONTROL IN ANY SITUATION — WHETHER WHEN LEADING HIM DOWN THE BARN AISLE, TAKING HIM TO TURNOUT, HANDLING HIM IN THE BREEDING SHED OR RIDING HIM AMONG MARES AND OTHER STALLIONS.

Boarding your big boy

Housing stallions can be a difficult proposition. Many boarding stables will not accept stallions. Others will board them but often with inadequate or unsafe facilities. Some stables have wonderful facilities but a staff inexperienced or improperly trained in handling stallions. Stables will usually charge a higher board rate for stallions, as much as 25 to 50 percent higher than for geldings or mares.

When evaluating a place to stable a stallion, pay close attention to the riding facilities. If the stable has a fenced area, is it used as a paddock or pasture to turn horses out? If so, you may find that the arena is full of horses every time you visit your horse, and you may find that you have no safe place to ride. **Stallions should not be ridden in an area where horses are running loose.** The risk of uncontrolled interaction between the stallion and the other horses is too great — either you or your stallion could easily get hurt.

Also, before you select a boarding stable, carefully interview the stable staff. These people will be handing your stallion every day.

If this mare was not interested in the stallion's attentions, she'd kick him. Most horses a stallion meets want to either kick or fight him, so a stallion often becomes aggressive — like the kid on the playground who bullies others so he doesn't get picked on.

Remember that a horse is always learning. If the staff handles him aggressively, he will react accordingly. If your stallion has been taught to lead properly, be sure the staff understands his training. They should not use a stud chain on a stallion who has been taught to lead properly, although many places use chains as standard practice. Be sure the staff will honor the rules you lay down regarding your horse's handling.

Housing him at home

Many people feel that keeping their stallion at home solves boarding-stable problems, but many small farms lack adequate facilities too. Wherever you stable your stallion, you must give careful consideration to his living quarters.

Like all horses, your stallion will need a stall or run-in shed as shelter from bad weather. If he is stalled in a barn with other horses, a sturdy, safe wall should separate him and the horse in the next stall. A solid wall between them is not necessary, but spacing between bars or rails should not allow the horses to get their head or feet trapped. The dividing wall should be high enough that neither horse can reach over the top. Ideally, the stall or shed will open into a large paddock.

The next consideration is a turnout area, which should be large enough to encourage him to exercise and graze. Turning a stallion into a round pen for a few hours a day is better than keeping him cooped up in a windowless stall all day, but a well-fenced pasture would be a much better option. **Make every effort to allow your stallion to live as natural a life as possible. He needs room to run and grass to graze.**

Fencing, then, is another major consideration. Fencing for a stallion should be 4½ to five feet tall, preferably electrified. This is especially true if the stallion can see other horses from his pasture. If the fence is not electrified, he may push against it to get closer to the other horses. Ideally, a 10-foot-wide (or wider) lane should separate the stallion pasture from other horse areas to prevent fighting over the fence and injury.

Fencing must not only keep your stallion in but also keep mares out. Many people do not realize how powerful a mare's desire to be bred can be. When a stallion is available, many mares will go to extreme measures to get to him. Mares have been known to run through gates and kick through board fences.

If at all possible, a stallion should be turned out with a companion horse. Horses are herd animals and to keep a stallion separated from his own kind is against his natural instincts. Many behavioral problems can be avoided or significantly reduced by giving a stallion a "roommate."

If you choose a mare for his companion, be sure she is large and bold enough to stand up to him when he gets cantankerous. Many people recommend turning out two mares, who will band together and easily control the stallion's actions. Avoid an overly aggressive mare, however, as she can inflict serious injury to a stallion, especially a young, inexperienced one.

Stallions can also be turned out with geldings, as long as no mares are on the property. If a nearby mare comes into heat, the stallion may attack his gelding buddy, in order to drive him away from the mare. Since the stallion has a much stronger urge to fight, the gelding can be injured or driven through the fence.

When keeping your stallion at home, you will also need to select a person to care for him when you are away. He or she must not be afraid of the horse, nor be determined to aggressively "show him who's boss." **It can be much more difficult to find a caregiver for your stallion than it would be for a mare or gelding.**

Stallions in social settings

There is no reason why a properly trained stallion can't be under control in any situation — whether when leading him down the barn aisle, taking him to turnout, handling him in the breeding shed or riding him among mares and other stallions. In these situations, the quality of his training will be put to the test. And, it takes work, time and a well-executed training plan to be able to control your stallion easily, without force and under almost all circumstances — but it is an attainable goal.

John expects Zip to exhibit good manners despite distractions.

The stallion owner's rule of thumb should be: The stallion should be so well-mannered that no one, except the horse's handler, should be aware that he is a stallion. The stallion's handler should keep him busy, focusing his attention on performance maneuvers to distract him from paying notice to the other horses.

In any situation where a stallion is present, it's the stallion handler's responsibility to watch out for the safety of those around him. If the stallion cannot be controlled, he should be removed from that situation immediately.

Often, stallion owners will go through an area announcing, "This is a stallion; please move away." People who feel everyone else must clear the way for their stallion are, at best, inconsiderate and, at worst, endangering other horses and riders. (However, until your stallion is under control, you may have to take special measures. If you need extra control, rather than using a chain lead shank, try using a full cheek snaffle with a lead rope attached to the left ring. That will give you more precise control of the horse's head without causing him pain. Of course, as when using a rein, you should never jerk on the lead rope.)

When riding in a group, a well-trained stallion should act much like a well-trained gelding. He should allow horses to come close to him on either side, bump him in the rump and walk in front of him, regardless of gender. **As a safety precaution, however, the stallion should not be allowed to sniff noses with another horse, because a stallion will often react by striking with a front foot.**

Biting — natural but not acceptable

No doubt about it — biting is natural behavior for a stallion. But just because a behavior comes naturally doesn't mean we have to live with it. And, since biting is a dangerous behavior, we have a responsibility to replace the undesirable behavior with behavior that we want. The best thing is to prevent the bite from happening, and there are four ways that I do this:

1. Give the horse more love and attention than he's looking for. *By "filling his bucket" with the right kind of attention, he's less likely to look for attention in all the wrong places. Generally speaking, the more you love on a stallion's head, the less is his tendency to bite. Owners who spend lots of time petting and loving on their stallion's head rarely have a horse who bites. The worst thing is to swat at the horse, which encourages him to come right back at you with his mouth.*

2. If the horse is mouthy, wanting to nibble on your shirt or whatever else is available, try positioning him out of reach of your shirt. *It may be that the temptation is just too strong. Train yourself (and him) to stand a few feet away from each other.*

3. When the horse's nose and mouth are close to you, rub his nose enthusiastically. *Keep rubbing until he takes his nose away. You don't want to hurt him — just bug him. When he brings his nose around again, rub it again. Most nosy horses are just looking for attention but wind up getting themselves in trouble.*

4. Use his behavior to remind you to work on something you want him to do better. *For example, when he gets too mouthy, ask him to step to the left, then to the right and so forth. Improve his halter manners. You are not punishing him, just putting his extra energy to work. Don't treat him roughly, but just give him a job to do. He'll determine that every time he gets mouthy, he has to work, so it's easier to keep his mouth to himself.*

If a horse actually bites — that is, if he opens his teeth even a little bit — I consider that an act of war. *Biting is the most dangerous thing a horse can do, and he's just declared war on me. I put it in my mind that I am going to kill that horse, and there are two rules of engagement:*

■ *I'm not allowed to hit the horse with anything that could cut or blind him. So for instance, a cotton lead rope would be fine to throw at his shoulder but not in his face.*

■ *I'm allowed to lose my temper — I can yell, scream, hit the horse and generally convince him he's going to die —* *but only for three seconds (one 1,000, two 1,000, three 1,000; cease fire). Then I have to pet the horse and act like the incident never happened.*

Some folks advocate putting a basket or muzzle on a horse. That's appropriate for some horses. But often, if a horse is really aggressive and can't get to you with his teeth, he'll sling his head into you or strike at you. A muzzle can limit your exposure to his teeth, but it won't train the horse.

In most cases when a horse bites, it's the handler's fault. The handler hasn't done enough training and handling to prevent him from biting. **PH**

Our thanks to contributing writer Kay Whittington

6

Proud Cut? Maybe Not.

A gelding who insists on acting like a stallion is often believed to be "proud cut." While this is sometimes true, it is still not an excuse for misbehavior.

You recently bought a gelding because they are reported to be easier to handle and more even-tempered than a mare or a stallion. You take the horse home, and on first spotting the other horses, he arches his neck, begins to prance and lets loose with an ear-splitting yell. In the field, he begins rounding up the mares and squaring off with the other geldings. A friend tells you he's definitely "proud cut." We'll look at what "proud cut" means and what else may be the cause of stallion-like behavior.

Characteristics of the proud-cut horse

The horse likely to be labeled as proud cut has the behavioral and physical characteristics of a stallion. Increased vocalization (loud neighing, whinnying) is a classic stallion trait usually lacking in geldings. The body type includes such things as heavy muscling and a pronounced arch/crest to the neck. Heavier muscling through the jowls of the face is also common. Stallions usually have less body fat, although this will be greatly influenced by feeding practices. The penis of a stallion or a horse gelded after sexual maturity will be larger than a horse who was gelded earlier.

Stallions have a higher energy level than geldings or mares, do more "prancing," are more alert and startle more easily. The level of aggression — striking, biting, pushing their way around — is usually higher for a stallion, but the level and effectiveness of training has such an important role to play here that an improperly trained mare or gelding could easily be more "aggressive" (really meaning out of control) than a well-handled stallion.

The most obvious distinction between stallions and geldings is how they react to a mare in season. Even horses with no other signs of male behavior may show a little interest in the mare but do not carry it beyond that point. True stallions, or geldings with retained stallion characteristics, will actively pursue the mare, engage in foreplay, achieve an erection and mount. However, the gelded or partially gelded horse is often unable to sustain the erection and actually breed the mare.

What is "proud cut"?

"Proud cut" means that when the horse was castrated, some of the tissue responsible for producing testosterone, the primary male hormone, was left in the horse. This is occasionally done intentionally, at the owner's request, to obtain a horse who retains much of the spark and physical characteristics of a stallion but without the ability to impregnate mares. In most cases, however, the tissue was inadvertently left behind. When castrations are done with the horse standing, problems — such as the horse moving, difficulty with accurately seeing the surgical site and controlling bleeding — can contribute to small amounts of hormone-producing tissue being left behind. Even under these conditions, however, the number of horses who are truly proud cut is fairly small. Horses may continue to display stallion characteristics for other reasons.

Cryptorchids

A cryptorchid is a horse who has one or both testicles located either high in the scrotum or retained inside the body. Such a horse may look like a gelding (no testicle can be seen or felt in the sac) and may even have castration scars from having had a normal testicle removed while the missing/hard-to-find one was left behind.

If an entire testicle is present, the horse is, for all intents and purposes, a stallion. He will produce sperm and will have all the stallion characteristics and stallion levels of hormones in his blood. He may or may not be fertile. If only part of a testicle remains, the horse will not be fertile but will most definitely be "proud cut."

Other causes of stallion-like behavior

For maximal behavior modification, horses are usually gelded before they reach sexual maturity (around 18 months). This is often simply a management decision, as young horses are usually kept in groups, and the horsey equivalent of teenagers with raging hormones can be disruptive. Also, allowing the male hormones to work for 12 to 18 months or so gives the horse the benefit of these powerful anabolic substances during the period of most rapid growth, so that most geldings are taller, heavier boned and more thickly muscled than most mares.

In addition to their physical effects, the male hormones influence the horse's "personality" — how he responds to life in general and specific social situations. They may also help determine the body's set-point for levels of other hormones and how much testosterone is produced from locations other than the testicles, such as the adrenal glands.

Stallions under the age of five are less physically mature and less confident than adults. This makes them easier to handle and often

This horse was gelded as an adult, about a year before this photo was taken. He still exhibits many stallion-like tendencies, but that is due to his habits, not his hormones. The owner is doing the right thing in telling him his boundaries.

leads inexperienced owners to think there really is not too much involved with managing and properly training a stallion. Castration may then be delayed until the horse matures and becomes more of a challenge.

Horses castrated after full physical maturity, for whatever reason, are far more likely to retain the physical and behavioral traits of a stallion to some degree. As a general rule, the later the castration, the more stallion-like the horse will remain. He may retain much of his heavier muscling for the remainder of his life. Interest in mares and in fighting with other males will drop off but may take months or years to disappear completely, if it ever does. Stallions who were very aggressive and difficult to handle may show little change in this aspect of their behavior, since it has its roots in poor training in the first place. Also, when horses are castrated later in life, you can expect it will take much longer for the physical and personality changes to occur.

Hormones or training?

Behaviors least likely to be affected by a successful surgical removal of hormone-producing tissues are those directly related to human-horse interactions. If the horse misbehaves in the barn or when being  *ridden, you have a training problem. "Bad" horses are made, not born. Male hormones are not excuses, or explanations, for horses who are difficult to handle. Decide honestly if you think you can, or want to, learn to effectively control the horse the way he is. If his behavior is more than you want to take on, sell him. If the horse has many desirable characteristics, work closely with a professional trainer. You will need to be actively involved in the horse's retraining, however, if you plan to handle him yourself.*

Determining if your horse is proud cut

It is often difficult, if not impossible, to tell if a horse has been proud cut or if he has just retained physical characteristics and behavior patterns from his days as a stallion. Blood tests can be done to check the levels of testosterone and estrogen. Estrogen is primarily a female hormone, but it is also present in high levels in stallions. It is often a more sensitive indicator of whether there is still active hormone-producing tissue in the body. If the horse is a cryptorchid, tests will show obviously elevated levels — the same as in stallions. If less tissue remains, results may not be as clear.

These tests can be difficult to interpret because of potential contributions to hormone levels by glands located elsewhere in the body. If you do have the tests done, locate an equine reproduction specialist at a veterinary school or university to get an expert opinion on the results.

If test results suggest the horse may indeed have been proud cut, surgery may not be the best option. Because the retained tissue is often small and scarring from the first castration great, it will be difficult for the surgeon or a pathologist examining the tissue to tell you for certain that the remaining pieces of gland were removed the second time. Surgery is also a major trauma for the horse, especially with general anesthesia.

The first step in dealing with a horse behaving as if he might be proud cut is to assess the situation and list exactly what it is about the horse that you cannot handle. If the major problem is related to his reaction to mares, fighting with other horses and trying to breed, it might be worthwhile to have hormone levels tested to determine if he is a cryptorchid or has smaller amounts of testicular tissue remaining.

You will have to work closely with your veterinarian and a reproduction expert to determine if surgery is likely to have an impact on the horse's behavior. Remember, too, that the older the horse is, the less likely even a successful surgery and lowering of hormone levels will have an impact on behavior. Many horses who were gelded late in life will lose the ability to breed but keep right on trying! PH

Notes

7

Cleaning The Sheath

Not all horseowners know that male horses —
both stallions and geldings — need help
with certain hygiene matters.
It's a messy job, but somebody has to do it.

Professional grooms think nothing of cleaning a sheath; it is routine. But for most novices and even some experienced horsemen, it's not routine because they don't know how to do it. We'll show you how to have a cleaner horse.

While the sheath is really just the pocket of skin around the penis, "sheath cleaning" includes cleaning both the inside of the horse's sheath and the penis. **Geldings and stallions not used for breeding should be cleaned once or twice a year.** Cleaning more often may cause dry, irritated skin.

Breeding stallions are generally washed as part of the breeding procedure when the penis is erect — this is easier because you can see what you are doing — but you'll still need to check and clean the pouch at the end of the penis once or twice a year.

Why do it?

Sheath cleaning removes smegma — the waxy or greasy secretions combined with dead skin cells that build up in the sheath. The secretions are normal; they are produced by glands in the lining of the sheath. **Smegma has a strong odor, and in some cases you can detect that a horse has a significant buildup by the odor alone.** Smegma also includes other dirt and bacteria, which may cause inflammation of the surrounding tissues.

Some horses accumulate more smegma than others — they throw dirt up on their bellies and sheaths because of the way they move; they live in dustier or dirtier environments; or they have pink skin, which may produce more smegma. (Wild horses probably got by without sheath cleaning because the penis of stallions more fully fills the sheath, and frequent erections naturally minimize dirt and smegma buildup.)

A buildup of smegma may cause the horse to rub his tail against his stall or a fence, but he may not appear otherwise uncomfortable. Horses who have recently been cleaned are more likely to extend their penis ("drop") more consistently and fully when they urinate. This enables them to direct the urine flow more accurately and avoid urinating on their hind legs.

Other benefits of sheath cleaning include opportunities to check for wounds, fly irritations, precancerous or cancerous lesions, and growths (like tumors, or melanomas, which are found in gray horses). Wounds may need an antibiotic ointment (like one of the yellow fura-ointments) applied until they heal.

Precancerous or cancerous lesions may be red, raw, ulcerated, angry-looking or irregular in shape. They are more prevalent on pink-skinned penises. **If a wound looks suspicious or does not respond to antibiotics, call your vet.**

Stand well out of kicking range, with your body close to the horse's, when cleaning the horse's sheath.

Even if your horse won't drop his penis, you can still feel for wounds or growths — if you have any question about their severity, consult your vet.

Most horses will have accumulated a mass of secretions in the blind pouch just above the urethra. This "bean" (so called because of its shape) is usually whitish or gray in color — sometimes in contrast to the darker color of the smegma in the rest of the sheath. The bean can be putty-like or harder in consistency and grows larger with time. It can obstruct the urethra, make the end of the penis painful to the touch (a problem in breeding stallions) and make urination painful.

Swollen sheaths

If the sheath is swollen, you can assume there is a good deal of inflammation and a heavy collection of material inside. Sheaths that appear to swell up overnight may have had insect irritation (i.e., a bee sting or large fly bite), chemical irritation or a wound. **Check carefully also for swelling along the belly since the swelling of belly and sheath could indicate a disease state rather than strictly a sheath problem.**

Sheaths that have not been cleaned in quite a while and become swollen may also contain adhesions — bands of scar tissue between the penis and surrounding tissues, or between the tissues themselves — that form as a result of irritation and possibly small tears in the skin. This will prevent the penis from being fully dropped.

Do not attempt to clean a swollen sheath unless the horse is tranquilized. *This is simply asking too much, as it is almost guaranteed to be sensitive. Wear a surgical glove or disposable latex exam glove over the rectal examination sleeve to avoid irritation to the interior of the sheath.*

Use K-Y jelly or another water-based lubricant to work your way around inside the sheath, removing large collections of material. These will rinse out readily. A small sponge (like a tack sponge) may help loosen adherent material. Use plenty of soap and warm water.

*Complete cleaning may take more than one session.
When you are not getting any further significant amount
of material, rinse thoroughly and pack the interior of the
sheath with either Furacin ointment or Nolvasan ointment to soften, soothe inflammation and fight bacteria.
Give the horse at least three days for the sheath to "quiet
down" before tranquilizing him again for a second examination and completion of cleaning.*

IF THE BUILDUP IS PARTICULARLY BAD,

COAT THE AREA LIBERALLY WITH BABY OIL

AND WAIT ONE DAY.

How do we do it?

While techniques vary, we recommend this economical and satis-
factory method.

Gather all your materials before you begin. Once you've started
you'll be too messy to go hunting for supplies. You don't have to stay
messy, and cleaning up is quick and easy if you get an arm-length
plastic palpation sleeve from your vet. Use a clothes pin to attach it
to your shirt, and you'll keep hand, arm and sleeve clean while you
work. When you're finished, turn it inside out as you remove it to
keep the mess inside. **If you choose not to use rubber gloves or a
sleeve, you'll find the smell stays on your skin a long time.**

Line a bucket with a clean plastic kitchen trash bag — the bag can
be discarded afterward, which is much easier than cleaning the
bucket. **When cleaning more than one horse, a different sleeve and
bucket liner should be used for each horse.** Fill the bucket with
comfortably warm water (please!) and enough iodine-based surgi-
cal/wound scrub to make a dark-tea-colored mixture. This is for lu-
bricating and rinsing your hand.

There are sheath-cleaning products on the market with specific
directions for their use. For years, mild soap, such as Ivory or
Castile, was the cleaner of choice — it is inexpensive and handy.
The difficulty with soap is that it may dry and irritate the skin;

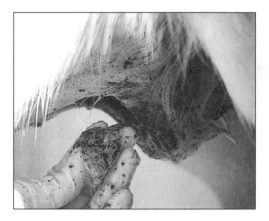

You'll want to be sure to wear rubber gloves, discarding them after use.

plus, particularly if the horse does not drop or stay dropped, it is difficult to rinse thoroughly.

Some horses will tolerate a stream of water directed by a garden hose into the sheath for rinsing (in warm weather!). However, if you miss any of the somewhat greasy smegma, it won't rinse off well.

Mineral oil, vegetable oil and petroleum jelly have been used, but they are rather thick and are not well absorbed by the skin, so dirt will collect readily in the newly cleaned sheath. We recommend baby oil. While it is not a cleaner, it works well to loosen and remove smegma and the bean. Because it is not an antibiotic, it won't upset the natural bacterial climate of the penis. Besides being non-irritating and moisturizing, it is absorbed by the skin without attracting dirt, and it lubricates our hand for easier access.

Some folks prefer to use cotton balls or sections of roll cotton to get the cleaner up into the sheath; we've found, however, that cotton fibers can get left behind (use each piece of cotton once and discard it). Rag or sponge pieces can be used the same way without the residue.

Wearing the palpation sleeve, dampen your hand and wrist in the iodine-water solution, then make a fist with your palm up, and pour oil liberally over your fingertips.

Step up to the horse's left side, rest your left arm over his back, and touch his belly in front of his sheath firmly with your right hand, leaving it in place until he accepts its presence. Then move your hand back to his sheath and insert your hand with your fingertips together and pointed upward. This initial touch is one that may elicit a response — a step away, a raised hind leg or a cow (forward) kick.

Staying well forward, out of hind-foot range, left hand over his back and your side against his, you can easily feel him prepare to kick or you can stay with him if he moves. If he steps away from you and gets away from the cleaning procedure, you've reinforced his avoidance. If, however, he finds that you will stay with him, he'll most likely stand still.

You can use a hose to rinse after cleaning the sheath, if you have access to warm water.

The next step is to loosen and remove the secretions inside the front of the sheath at the abdominal wall. This is where the baby oil comes in handy — it gently loosens the secretions. Start gently and, as you find the horse will tolerate it, scrub with your fingers. Then, move inside along the sheath. To gauge his response, clean the far (right) side of the sheath first. If he is going to be bothered by it and kick, often he will kick with his right hoof and miss you. If you are gentle — and he is tolerant — by the time you get to the left side, he will have accepted the procedure.

Rinse your hand in the iodine-water solution periodically. Reapply baby oil and continue. **Be sure to place the bucket and baby oil container a safe distance away from the horse, so that reaching into it does not put you in the path of a front or hind hoof.**

If the buildup is particularly bad in any part of the sheath, coat the area liberally with baby oil and wait one day. The smegma will be softened and less irritating to remove.

Once you have cleaned all accumulated secretions from the abdominal wall and the sides of that part of the sheath, move into the inner cavity. Access to the inner cavity is through a ring of tissue. If by now the horse has relaxed and dropped his penis, your work is much easier. If not, you'll eventually be wrist deep in the inner cavity, but it is still possible to do a thorough job.

There is no reason to forcibly pull the penis out of the sheath — the horse is likely to react violently, and you might even damage the penis. As you move upward along the relaxed and retracted penis, you will find many folds of skin that would smooth out if the penis was extended. Along the length of the penis you will probably find long scales of dry material. The baby oil will soften the attachment and allow them to be slipped off. Continue gently rubbing oil into the skin and rubbing the secretions off. Work all the way around the penis.

Restrain the horse

Assuming the horse has been taught to stand tied, we suggest tying him high, so the knot won't slip down. Other forms of restraint, such as having an assistant hold the horse or cross-tying him, allow more forward movement, which can put you within kicking range of the hind hoof. However, some horses tolerate sheath cleaning better when held. It is sometimes helpful if you can position the horse between you and a wall or fence — this keeps him from moving away from you.

Some horses find this procedure irritating no matter how carefully it's done, and because of the danger to the handler from a well-aimed kick, choose a time and place where cooperation is likely. A warm, sunny, lazy afternoon, or during normal grooming time after a workout, is more likely to lead to success than the time when a horse is full of energy and you've just turned his buddy out to play.

You might be successful if you start after he has dropped to urinate — but don't be daunted if he feels pressure and retracts his penis. With gentle handling, you may be able to get him to relax and drop again. (Some folks report that scratching the horse's belly just along the midline is a help.)

During the sheath-cleaning procedure, we've had horses raise their hind leg in warning, had them kick at their sheaths (to chase off the irritant), had them kick toward us. The zealous ones even aim fairly accurately toward us and mean it. We often find that, after the initial touch, even a horse who has just kicked will quiet down and allow himself to be cleaned when he realizes the procedure does not hurt.

*You be the judge — if the horse objects strenuously, it's better to wait with the cleaning procedure until you can have a vet sedate him. **An advantage of tranquilization is that often the horse will relax and allow his penis to drop, giving you a chance to see what you are doing.***

The bean

Leave bean removal for last because by this time you have had a chance to gauge the horse's reactions and he has had a chance to learn that the procedure does not hurt. At the end of the penis, the urethral opening protrudes slightly. The opening above the urethra (anatomically, the *fossa navicularis*) can be quite small, so it helps if you have small fingers.

Looking at the penis from the urethral opening, or feeling it if necessary, you will notice that the higher opening is horizontal. **If a bean is present and it's small and soft enough, you can probably scoop it out with your finger.** If not, break it in half — or in pieces — from the center part (which is easier to reach) and remove a piece at a time.

This can be painful, particularly if the bean is large and hard, so be alert for a kick. Even if the horse's penis is retracted, if you are standing close enough to the horse, his stifle will push you away before his hoof is raised much off the ground. Once the bean is fragmented, the discomfort lessens, and some horses will cease to object. **If the bean is too large and hard, or the horse objects too strenuously, asking your veterinarian to tranquilize the horse can make the procedure safer and quicker.**

Cleaning the sheath once or twice a year to remove smegma before it builds up and removing the bean before it gets large will keep the procedure more comfortable for the horse and easier for you. ■PH

Our thanks to contributing writer Sue Stuska, Ed.D.

8

Getting Along With Mares

Mares have a reputation for being cantankerous, inconsistent, moody and difficult to handle. What can you do to get along better with your mare?

How a mare responds to people is a complex interaction between her instincts, her experience with other horses, her individual personality and even hormonal factors. While each horse is an individual, you can use a few rules of thumb to understand mares' behavior and form a better relationship with them.

If you were to compare horses to pets, then geldings and stallions would be more like dogs while mares would be like cats. **Mares are less physically interactive with people until, and unless, they have accepted the individual as having a rightful place in their world.** On first meeting a mare, you are likely to get the "I couldn't care less about your existence" impression. This is more indifference than hostility, although people often take it personally. If you force the issue, the mare will either tolerate your touch or pin her ears and walk away. The best you usually get on first contact with a mare is a noncommittal response.

Although this definitely qualifies as cat-like behavior, it is very much female horse behavior and something you should become familiar with. Mares are social animals, equipped with responses that serve them well in the group. Had you been another horse, she would have faced you squarely, sniffed for a few moments, then either squealed in aggression (the back-off-or-else message), turned and walked away (the you-follow-me message) or dropped her head to graze (the you're-OK-with-me message to an equal).

Mares are generally more cautious than geldings, and it may take more effort and consistency to develop a trusting relationship. Handle them in a simple, straightforward, but tactful, way.

Gaining a mare's acceptance, trust and affection is a procedure that cannot be rushed. You may be able to keep her attention by plying her with favorite treats, but you will not get anywhere by fussing around her, patting her, talking to her or otherwise making a pest out of yourself. The way to work your way into her world is to deal with her quietly and consistently, keep to as close a schedule as possible and perform tasks in a predictable ritual — food comes at such and such a time, work is preceded by hoof picking and grooming (always with the same brushes, used in the same order), tacking up, work, untacking, bath or grooming and so forth. All horses appreciate order in their world, but this is especially true of mares.

It goes without saying that all horses should be handled with kindness. Imperfect beings that we are, however, we are bound to have days when we are worried or preoccupied and our tempers are short. Geldings and stallions are much more forgiving of this behavior than are mares. A mare will remember any mistreatment for a long time, perhaps indefinitely. This is an important trait to have when trying to coexist in a band. The mare needs to remember which individuals to steer clear of.

Mares also pick up on your displeasure more quickly than geldings or stallions. A sharp word may be all it takes to get a mare's attention if she is doing something you disprove of. It's not that mares are more "sensitive" per se; they are more tuned in to everything around them — again, a valuable trait for self-preservation in the band.

On the flip side is when your mare is having a bad day. She may be in the midst of hormonal changes or simply may not be herself. (The boys get like this sometimes, too!) **You should not let a mare have her own way simply because she is out of sorts (although it would be wise to recognize the problem before you get into a full-scale battle).** Keep your expectations and demands fairly simple to make it more likely that you'll end the session on a good note. What you should be aware of is that a mare in a bad mood can be genuinely dangerous.

Mares in the wild

Position in the band — Many of what we would call problem behaviors or difficult personality traits in mares have their roots in band, or herd, behavior. The stallion's role is quite simple. He breeds, stands guard, warns of danger and fights if need be — not that mares can't hold their own in physical encounters, as many a stallion who tried his luck with a mare too early in her estrus cycle could tell you. There is little social interchange between mares and stallions otherwise. He is a fairly solitary creature.

The picture with mares is different. Mares care for the young and so remain in fairly close physical contact with other mares. This unity provides strength in numbers to the band in the event of an attack. It also can lead to the tensions inherent in any crowding situation, and a rigid social structure exists to keep conflicts at a minimum.

The "alpha mare" is the queen. She keeps the band together and determines where they will graze, when they seek water and when it is time to move on. Her authority is absolute, and any who attempt to go their own way are dealt with severely. She is a dictator, not a diplomat, and wields more authority with the mares than the stallion does.

Below the alpha mare is a subtle hierarchy, a pecking order. Other physically strong, strong-willed mares are next in line. They drink first, move along when traveling at the front of the band and get their pick of grazing locations. Spats break out from time to time among these mares and serve to determine exactly who is No. 2, No. 3, etc. Social position within the band drops for mares who are younger, weaker and less aggressive.

Mares in a similar position in the pecking order "hang out" together in small groups of two or three. Most miserable is the newcomer. Unless she is a particularly dominant mare, the newcomer will usually be a social outcast, existing on the fringes of the band, edging her way toward one or another of the groups of lower-caste mares, in hopes one will welcome her in. This process of acceptance can take days or weeks.

Motherly love *— Insight into the psyche of mares can also be obtained by watching their behavior with their foals. With few exceptions, mares with foals younger than one week old are extremely vigilant and protective. It is not at all unusual for a mare to refuse to allow any other horse to get near her foal during this time. It will often take at least a month before the mare is comfortable allowing the foal more than a few feet away from her.*

Mares "talk" to their babies in low, deep tones, different from the yells you are accustomed to hearing at feeding time or the whinnying between buddies. When directing the youngster to stand or nurse, they use gentle but relentless persuasion, nudging and pushing the foal in the desired direction.

As the foal gets older and begins to get his own ideas, the mare's behavior changes and protectiveness diminishes. The mare also begins to move into a much more no-nonsense attitude about directing the foal.

The foal who gets overly rambunctious, too rough nursing or dares to kick or bite the mare will be swiftly disciplined, usually with a bite on the neck. Some mares even keep foals away from hay and grain at feeding time. What might look like "meanness" is really teaching the foal two valuable lessons — "respect your elders" (the others are likely to deal with him even more harshly) and "you have to learn to fend for yourself."

She doesn't kid around

Mares don't bluff. If a mare is pinning her ears and swishing her tail, she means business. Don't position yourself where you can be kicked, struck or bitten. A well-trained mare can be reminded quickly who is in charge and will give in — grudgingly, probably, but she will cooperate.

Don't make the mistake of "being nice" to her when she acts aggressively. Attention from you is likely the last thing she is looking for, and your "niceness" could be taken for weakness, encouraging her to resist even more. The mare who resists handling or working will likely respond and react much the same as she would in a similar situation with a band of horses. If she feels she is higher in the pecking order, she will fight to have her way. This is how she restores social order to her world, vanquishing the offender — in this case, you!

Complicating your relationship with the mare will be her social position with other horses. The alpha/dominant mare may react in two general ways to the humans in her life. She may transfer all that vibrant energy and self confidence into being an exceptional performer. Properly handled, this will usually be the case. If not

All this mare-ish behavior has benefits. When you see a mare with her foal, you marvel at the extent of her motherly wisdom.

properly handled, however, all the aggression and power in her personality will be directed at resisting you. You can also expect that even a usually cooperative alpha mare will have her moments. When she is being bad, she will be VERY bad!

Mares at the lower end of the pecking order can often be more difficult to deal with than alpha types. These mares have had a lifetime of being submissive and passive and are often just waiting for their chance to throw their weight around. They know there are unpleasant physical consequences for ignoring the authority of an alpha mare — and you are probably nowhere near as intimidating. Many people have been astonished to see how their aggressive and difficult-to-manage mare transforms into a lamb when turned out with other mares. To get control, you must assume the role of alpha mare when handling her. Establish control with careful training; never put yourself in a position where you cannot readily establish control. Be firm, but never abusive.

Mares who have been dominated by other mares may also be a real problem in the field if turned out with geldings — ripping off blankets, kicking, biting, hogging all the hay or grain, insisting on being first to be brought in and so forth. The same thing happens when these mares take out their frustrations on their owners. Very few geldings or stallions will defend themselves from a mare (they instinctively don't hit ladies!), and her reign of terror will likely continue indefinitely.

When it's all worthwhile

Establishing a relationship with a mare is definitely more difficult than with a gelding. It is also definitely worth the effort. Mares become very attached to the special people in their lives, showing affection by rubbing, nuzzling, "talking" and even licking! They will look for you in a crowd (like at a show) and whinny in recognition when they see you coming. Their trust, once you earn it, is complete and rewarding. ■PH■

9

Mares In Heat

*Understanding your mare's estrus cycles
can reduce frustration when
Mrs. Jekyll turns into Mrs. Hyde.*

The horse's need to reproduce and preserve its species is, as in other species, one of its most powerful drives. Therefore, it should come as no surprise that during those times of her cycle when she is able to become pregnant a mare is preoccupied with her relationship with other horses and is not focused on her owner or rider. **Estrus, or "heat," lasts between two to 10 days, with six days being the average.** After the mare has ovulated (released a mature egg from her ovary), estrus ends rapidly, within one or two days. We'll look first at the estrus cycle itself and how it works. Then we'll look at the mare's behavior and consider how to deal with it. Finally we'll look at the effectiveness of progesterone therapy.

The estrus cycle

Horses are considered to be "seasonally polyestrus," meaning that at certain seasons of the year they have multiple estrus cycles. Both mares and stallions show seasonal variations in their sexual behavior, but the changes are more marked and more noticeable to us, in mares.

Beginning in late winter or early spring, sometimes as early as February, the mare's ovaries begin to show signs of activity. This process is triggered by increasingly long periods of daylight. The

During breeding season, mares often have heightened awareness of both horses and people around them and may have difficulty focusing on the requests of their riders and owners.

longer days are sensed by the pineal (pronounced pine-E-ul) gland in the brain. The brain then decreases its secretion of the melatonin hormone, which you may recognize as the hormone everyone is now raving about for treatment of jet lag and other sleep disorders.

As melatonin levels fall off, the pituitary gland (the "master gland" of the body, which controls all hormonal systems) is signaled by the hypothalamus, another part of the brain, to begin the process of stimulating the mare's ovaries to produce follicles.

Breeding season extends from late spring through early fall, peaking in the warmest months of the year. Since the mare carries her foal for an average of about 340 days, just over 11 months, most foals are born at the most opportune time, when both general weather conditions and quality of pastures are highly favorable.

The percentage of mares showing obvious estral cycles is highest in the summer months. During this time, cycling will occur at intervals that are regular and predictable. Individual mares, however, vary in the length of their cycles, which can range anywhere from 18 to 24 days.

If you are tracking your mare's cycle, you should count days by beginning at a specific point in the cycle. For example, if the time when the mare is willing to stand still to be bred is "day 0," this behavior will reappear between days 18 and 24, depending on the mare's cycle. A more precise measurement might be made by a veterinarian on the basis of a rectal examination to determine exactly when the mare has ovulated. Again, ovulation would reoccur between days 18 and 24 — unless, of course, the mare is bred and becomes pregnant.

Hormones and the estrus cycle

At either end of the breeding season (late spring or early fall), sexual behavior is erratic. Cycle lengths may be very long or very short, with little predictability. Some mares show typical sexual behavior (as we'll discuss), but others may show nothing or only slight, ill-defined changes in behavior. This is because the hormones controlling the estral cycle are not being secreted in peak amounts. Certain stages of the cycle may be prolonged, shortened or simply missed.

We already mentioned some of the hormones originating in the brain that play a role in estrus. As melatonin levels fall off, the hypothalamus increases its secretion of a hormone called "gonadotropin-releasing hormone," which stimulates the sex organs by signaling the pituitary gland that conditions are right to begin releasing gonado-tropins — specifically, the follicle-stimulating hormone (FSH). See the graph on page 82.

Follicle development

Follicles are structures on the ovary destined to produce a mature egg cell. Under the influence of FSH, one or more follicles on the mare's ovary will begin to enlarge and grow. Ultimately, only one of these will continue developing, and any others will regress. **As this follicle grows, it produces increasing amounts of estrogen, the "female" hormone.** Under the influence of estrogen, the cervix begins to relax and spread out and secretions along the reproductive tract increase. As the follicle approaches maturation, levels of estrogen are at their peak, sexual activity begins to occur, and the mare starts to show signs of being in heat.

The high levels of estrogen signal the pituitary gland to stop secreting the follicle-stimulating hormone and begin production of another type of gonadotropic hormone, called "luteinizing hormone," or LH.

Luteinizing hormone stimulates ovulation, the release of the egg. After the mare has ovulated, the follicle collapses, becoming a *corpus luteum* (Latin for what it looks like, "yellow body"), and begins to develop a type of cell producing the progesterone hormone.

Estrogen drops as progesterone rises, and the mare stops being receptive to the stallion. Progesterone prepares the uterus for implantation of a pregnancy by increasing the blood supply to it and causes the cervix to become tighter and firmer, closing off the uterus from the vagina and the outside world. Secretions along the reproductive tract also become thicker and more tenacious, further helping to seal off the uterus by forming a thick, mucus plug at the opening of the cervix.

If pregnancy does not occur, the corpus luteum will shrink under the influence of yet another hormone, prostaglandin, secreted by the uterus. A drop in progesterone in turn triggers FSH release, and the process begins all over again.

Behavior during estrus

While mares' estral behavior may be dramatic or relatively mild, an individual mare generally acts the same from cycle to cycle.

In early stages of estrus, many mares become "touchy." They may overreact to noise or a hand on their body, becoming startled easily. Signs of irritability, such as ear pinning, teeth baring, kicking or threatening to kick, and tail swishing, are common. These behaviors are especially pronounced, understandably, when another horse is around. During this time, the mare will not accept the sexual advances of a stallion, reacting even violently to him, though in a day or so the picture will be different.

As ovulation approaches, the mare becomes more and more receptive to breeding. Mares "signal" to other horses by raising their tail, by squirting small amounts of urine (which, one surmises correctly, contains a pheromone noteworthy to the stallion) and by repeatedly opening and closing the vulva (referred to as "winking"). When in the presence of a stallion, or even a gelding, the mare may

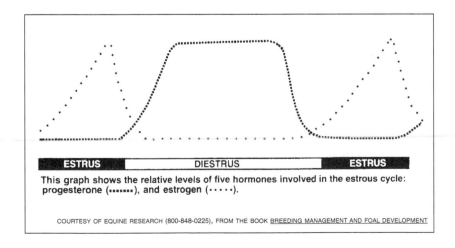

| ESTRUS | DIESTRUS | ESTRUS |

This graph shows the relative levels of five hormones involved in the estrous cycle: progesterone (••••••••), and estrogen (•••••).

COURTESY OF EQUINE RESEARCH (800-848-0225), FROM THE BOOK BREEDING MANAGEMENT AND FOAL DEVELOPMENT

squirt urine almost constantly and may stand squarely, being reluctant or refusing to move, in anticipation of being mounted.

During this time of peak receptivity, the mare's attention is on more important things than the people around her. She will seek the company of other horses and may be less than enthusiastic about anything you have planned for her to do.

After ovulating, receptivity to the stallion will persist for only a short period, sometimes as brief as 12 hours. Then there is rapidly rising resistance to the stallion, and many mares become as irritable as they were in early estrus.

Mares will vary in how strongly they exhibit signs of estrus, as well as in what those signs may be. While the period of receptivity, winking, squirting urine, etc. are fairly constant behaviors in most mares, how they react early and late in the estrus, as well as how they react to people, can be very different. Some mares are very irritable and extremely resistant to everything from grooming to being worked. Others become dull, listless and poorly responsive. Regardless of how the mare reacts, one thing is certain: Dramatic behavior fluctuations during estrus can interfere with performance under saddle and barn routine.

Dealing with the mare in estrus

How one reacts to the challenge of dealing with a mare in heat depends considerably on the relationship they have already established with the mare and on the relationship they generally expect horses to have with their owners. If, for example, you are expecting a horse to show qualities like loyalty and devotion, you're apt to be disappointed with your mare when she is in estrus. Although a bond between horse and owner may be strong, it is never as strong as horse to horse if your horse is normal, particularly at this point, which is the only way it could be if the species is to be preserved.

While few people would presume to think a mare would desire to leave her foal to share her rider's company, it is also unrealistic to think the mare at her limited time of peak fertility for the year will banish thoughts of breeding and be as responsive to humans as at other times.

However, if you accept the fact you will not always be priority No. 1 to your mare, there are things you can do to minimize difficulties. The foremost of these is to not overreact. **The mare's irritability, for instance, is not directed at you personally. If you learn to recognize those things that are most likely to irritate her (i.e.,**

Other horses instinctively know a mare means business when she threatens — so a physical confrontation is rarely necessary.

approaching from behind, touching the hindquarters) and try to avoid them, you will have made a great beginning.

Observe the mare and note which things in her behavior can be ignored and which must be handled. For example, swishing her tail frequently may annoy you, but it's probably harmless. Even ear pinning, while unattractive, may at times safely be ignored, often stopping within seconds anyway.

Behavior problems

Teeth baring and threats to bite or kick are serious and will likely get out of hand if you don't take notice and act. It is never appropriate for a horse to bite or threaten to bite a person. In these instances, the mare should not get any special consideration simply because she is in estrus.

But there are some aspects of estral behavior you are not likely to influence. They are instinctive. These include squirting urine and winking. If the mare is in the presence of a stallion or a particularly "studdish" gelding, some expression of this behavior is virtually inevitable. During the receptive phase of estrus, the mare is very strongly attracted to a potential mate.

Fortunately, a trait common to all horses will help you even during peak receptivity: They have trouble concentrating on more than one thing at a time. If you cannot easily minimize the proximity to any horse she finds overwhelmingly attractive, keep the mare distracted with things that are interesting but not too demanding. Some mares might even cease estral behavior as you're doing this.

Handling a mare in "heat" can be similar to handling a stallion and can be dangerous in some circumstances. You must insist on the animal's full attention and be alert for distractions strong enough to cause her to lose that focus.

It's not uncommon for a mare to yell in your ear as you walk her down the barn aisle, stomp a foot or prance from excitement but not resistance. Overreacting to minor misbehaviors such as these may ultimately make matters worse by constantly irritating the mare with corrections she does not really clearly understand. On the other hand, clear boundaries must be set so that the horse understands there are certain things that are never acceptable, such as kicking, biting and attempting to break free.

One other important distinction to realize about mares is that they don't make idle threats. Stallions may flex their neck or pretend to be ready to strike and so forth as a form of play. Their handlers learn to distinguish a stallion's play from true aggression, but mares do not play in this fashion. If a mare is showing dramatic behavior changes, her resistance to you may be quite forceful. Don't put yourself in a position where you could get hurt.

An attempt to force your will on a mare is not likely to meet with success. A mare who violently resists doing something is not testing your will. If you attempt to force the issue, she will likely fight back.

There's no question that hormonal changes affect the performance of some mares, making them more successful campaigners in the winter than in late spring and summer.

For example, a mare in "heat" may refuse to face you when you enter the stall, standing head in the corner with ears pinned back. A mare doing this is clearly saying, "Don't bother me now." A stallion exhibiting this behavior is saying, "Make me." If you simply stand still, the stallion may move on to something more aggressive, such as swinging his hindquarters or threatening to kick, but the mare will either do nothing else or will turn around to face you. So, check out the feed tub or leave briefly and come back. Forcing the issue will not do you any good.

This is when having taught your mare ground manners and specific cues will pay off. If you've conditioned her to respond to your cues (by being consistent and doing the thousands of repetitions we've talked about), she will not get herself into trouble and perhaps endanger you.

Is progesterone the answer for mare behavior problems?

Since progesterone is the "pregnancy hormone" whose rise triggers the end of estral behaviors in mares, why not fool Mother Nature by giving progesterone to mares in heat? Many people, especially with competition horses, put their mares on progesterone (usually in the oral form, but sometimes with injections) to eliminate problems associated with the mare's being in estrus, but is this the best answer?

Progesterone use may be a reasonable approach for mares whose behavior is truly unmanageable when they are in heat, or in the case of an important show or other competition that coincides with the mare's estrus, but you should discuss this fully with your veterinarian.

Treatment appears to be relatively free of side effects, at least with the oral form of progesterone, although a negative impact on the mare's ability to cycle normally after long periods of progesterone administration is always a possibility, which can be a problem if you are planning to breed the mare. There are no long-term studies on other possible side effects.

Do mares get PMS? — *Premenstrual syndrome (PMS) does not really apply to mares since they do not menstruate. However, they do experience hormonal ups and downs as do humans and other mammals.*

PMS in humans occurs during the stage of the cycle when estrogen levels are dropping and progesterone is rising. Progesterone is also at very high levels during pregnancy and contributes to such problems as excessive weight gain, fatigue, water retention and emotional instability.

Estrogen, on the other hand, is associated with a sense of well-being and high energy. It is used in menopausal ("change of life") women, for whom it is very useful, and in preventing heart disease and osteoporosis (bone loss that causes bones to become brittle and easily broken in older people).

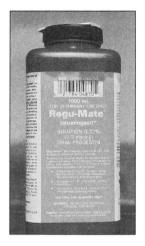

In mares, estrogen levels rise gradually in the 10 days or so preceding estrus, peak before ovulation and drop after that. Progesterone levels begin to rise after the mare has stopped showing signs of estrus and peak about 10 days thereafter.

Many people want to put their mares on progesterone in hopes it will lead to a better disposition and/or improved performance. When you realize progesterone is Regu-Mate®, available through veterinarians, suppresses heat in mares. *the hormone associated with pregnancy and PMS, you can see that the effect may not be quite what they had in mind! You will be able to get some idea of the effect that progesterone treatment will have on your mare by carefully plotting her disposition, general attitude and willingness to work over one or two cycles. If you find she is happier and more willing in the week or so preceding her estrus than she is for the week to 10 days afterward, progesterone is definitely something you want to avoid.*

Alternatives *— Before reaching for this, or any other potent drug, examine the whole situation carefully. Are there areas in your training that need to be strengthened? Imperfections in your relationship with the horse are likely to be magnified when she is in estrus and will, conversely, greatly improve the situation when they are corrected.*

Are you reacting to what are really perfectly normal, not exaggerated, responses? If irritability or aggressiveness is the problem, consider getting advice on ways to minimize this with training to keep the mare's attention and provide her with adequate amounts of exercise with proper breaks.

Try to avoid introducing new tasks or demanding work at those times when the mare is not focused on performance. It is interesting to note that high-performance mares involved in activities such as racing, eventing and showing on a regular basis often do not present as much of a problem during estrus as mares with an easier, laid-back existence — at least during the time they are working. While hormone therapy is effective in many cases, it should not be the first step. **PH**

10

Body Talk

*Horses' body language speaks to us loud and clear.
Understanding it may help keep us
safer and our horses happier and healthier.*

ll horseowners have wished at some time or another that their horses could talk. Fact is, while language skills are definitely lacking, horses do communicate with us, if we know what to watch for.

Look at that face

It is often said the eyes are the windows to the soul. This works in horses, too. The most well-recognized eye signal is the "wild-eyed," "crazy-eyed" or "white-eyed" look. This means that when you look at the horse's eye, you can see the white portion (sclera) that is usually encased in the eye lids and socket and not visible.

In some cases this is simply caused by the lids and/or eye socket being slightly too small for the size of the eye. These horses are often unjustly labeled as unruly. **Most times, however, the whites of the eyes show when the horse is excited.** Fear, aggression or agitation causes a release of adrenalin that energizes the horse, dilates the pupils and makes the lids pull wide open.

A horse in this state is either ready to make a quick move in response to something that upsets him or has a plan of action and is waiting for the correct moment to play it out. The horse may have heard an unsettling noise, seen a movement he considered a possible threat or spotted you coming with a tube of deworming paste!

Whatever it is that lies behind that white-eyed look, be warned that the horse is primed and ready to make an evasive, aggressive or resistant move.

We see other eye expressions so often we fail to notice them. As above, the pleasantly excited horse will also have dilated pupils (return of a buddy, dinner time, etc.). The happy and excited horse, however, usually will not show the whites of his eyes.

Eyes with lids partially closed mean the same thing they do in people — the horse is dozing, relaxed or possibly lost in thought.

One of the most eloquent looks that horses can get — and one that seems to belong only to exceptional horses — is the "look of champions." You can often catch some horses standing perfectly still but looking alert, head high, staring intensely off into the distance with a far-away look in their eyes. Stallions are the most likely to strike this pose, and it perfectly reflects their strength, animation and power.

Another expressive look is the soft gaze a mare will show her foal. It is often accompanied by a small nuzzle and a low-pitched nicker. This is a special look of affection, and if you are lucky enough to receive this type of a greeting yourself, you should feel very honored indeed!

A horse's ears also indicate how he feels. We all know that pinned ears often mean the horse is irritated. The flatter to the head the ears are pinned, the more intense is the horse's anger. Horses will also often pin their ears when they are concentrating on a difficult task, as when racing or moving a steer, and will pin their ears if there is a sound detected behind them.

The reverse — pricked ears — means the horse is focused on something interesting. If you look carefully, you will be able to see the

This horse isn't keeping it a secret that he's annoyed. His stiff neck and the expression of his eyes and ears tell us he is perturbed with something or someone behind him and he's ready to launch a kick.

Upon smelling something new, horses often exhibit the Flehman response. This may be their way of cataloging the smell for later recognition. It is frequently done after another horse urinates.

difference between ears that are truly pricked forward and those that are simply in the neutral, happy or nothing-in-particular-is-going-on-right-now position.

Pricked ears and dilated pupils from interest or pleasure go together; flat-back ears and whites of the eyes are a common pair. If you see the whites of the eyes and ears pricked forward, watch out — that horse is likely to make a move at any moment.

Some horses are also expressive with their nose and lips. Young animals and an occasional particularly gregarious older horse will use the nose/muzzle in exploratory play, contracting all the muscles until the muzzle and upper lip area take on an exaggerated, almost beak-like appearance, then wiggling it back and forth in the direction of their object of interest.

Horses curl their upper lips when a smell or taste gets their attention. It may signal pleasure (after a stallion has sniffed a mare) or register distrust or disgust (after smelling or tasting medicated or supplemented feed). This is usually done with the nose pointed up in the air, and whites of the eyes may appear, although this is more a function of the position of the head than anything else.

One peculiar mouth motion that only young foals make is a series of rapid chewing movements. Weanlings, and sometimes even yearlings, frequently do this when introduced to a new horse. It is not clear what this means — a simple "Hi," an "I would like to nurse" or some form of nervousness unique to babies. In any event, it is an effective signal to the other horse that this is an immature animal who does not pose a threat. It may also be an expression of submission.

Some horses — the outgoing and slightly clownish type — seem to be orally fixated. A favorite game is to hang their tongue out the side of their mouth, inviting and daring you to catch it. This is somewhat more common in horses who have been on the racetrack at some time (grooms often encourage this type of play). **Generally speaking, it is a trait of horses who are good natured but have a lot of energy and are constantly looking for ways to interact.**

Nuzzling is the horse's way of giving you a hug. It is a sign of affection that is not often seen between mature horses but is common between mares and foals. Nuzzling is also a gentle way of getting your attention, and mares do the same with their foals. **Be forewarned, however, nuzzling that is ignored will turn to more forceful nudging and from that to a flat-out head butt until the nuzzlee pays attention.**

Sniffing is one of the horse's ways of exploring his environment, including the humans and animals in it. Sometimes horses seem to enjoy sniffing objects, people or animals they know well, enjoying the familiar smell. Sniffing is also part of the ritual when a horse meets a new horse. The strangers will stand facing each other, touch noses sniffing and then slowly sniff farther back along the neck toward the withers.

Dealing with unwanted behaviors

Rather than hitting or yelling at the horse who is stomping his feet, pinning his ears or pawing, you have more effective options. In most cases, you are dealing with two factors. One is training the horse's emotions — he must learn patience. The other is teaching the horse what you want him to do.

If the horse is just doing attention-demanding movements, such as pawing when standing tied, you can try ignoring his behavior. If he sees that pawing doesn't merit any attention, positive or negative, then he quits putting out effort pawing.

The second technique is to replace the behavior you don't want with behavior you do want. So, let's say the horse is on a lead line. Each time he stomps his foot, ask him to step back three steps, then to the left three steps, then to the right three steps, then forward to the original place he was standing. You may have to do this routine a number of times, but eventually the horse will recognize that you "reward" his stomping behavior with work, and he'll quit stomping. In the meanwhile, you haven't created any additional unwanted behaviors (such as him raising his head if you jerked on the lead line), and you've improved his responsiveness to the WESN lesson.

Sometimes the solution is as simple as removing the occasion for a horse to get into trouble and teaching him what you want him to do. If your horse is a "nudger," always nuzzling you and bumping into your arm as you talk with other people at the barn, teach him to stand three feet away from you. Each time he comes closer than you want, give him a job to do, as we just described for the horse who stomps his feet. After a few tries, he'll get the idea that you want him to stand three feet away.

Chronic ear-pinning is a danger sign because the behavior that follows is often biting. You want to change your horse's attitude before ear-pinning gets to that stage. Ask yourself what you can do to get your horse's ears up, then build a lesson plan on that.

For instance, let's say your horse is in his stall and looks grumpy (not aggressive, just ears-back grumpy). Start tapping lightly on the stall door. Keep tapping as long as his ears are back. The moment he flicks an ear forward for any reason, stop tapping. With consistency, he'll realize

Consistent training on the lead will result in a horse with good ground manners who is a pleasure to work around.

that you bug him (by tapping on the door) when his ears look grumpy and that you quit bugging him when his ears look happy. You'll have developed a cue to tell him to change his thinking. When you change the position of the horse's ears, you change the thoughts running through his head.

The neck

Neck position is also a communication tool. A long, relaxed neck with the head in a low position means the horse is dozing or taking it easy.

A raised neck and elevated head indicate the horse is alert and/or focusing intently. Arching the neck is something we usually associate with stallions and is their way of "flexing their pecs." Mares and geldings, however, will also show neck arching when they are in the exploratory phase of meeting a new horse or any time they are exploring something in their environment that is unfamiliar and considered possibly dangerous — from a dog to a particularly threatening-appearing piece of paper on the trail.

Horses who are wrapped up in what they are doing, in this case racing each other around the paddock, will often have their ears pinned, even when they are thoroughly enjoying themselves.

The tail

Horses clearly make their thinking known with their tails. They are similar to cats in that rapid swishing of the tail signals irritation. An arched tail is the hallmark of the horse who is feeling particularly full of himself and is commonly seen when horses are turned out after stall confinement or are prancing under saddle.

The tightly clamped tail occurs when the horse is irritated or feels threatened by something going on around his hindquarters, whether it is a brush going in an uncomfortable direction or the approach of a human or another animal. The tightly clamped tail is a clear warning to watch out — next step is a kick.

THE TIED-UP HORSE WILL AVOID PUTTING WEIGHT ON HIS HINDQUARTERS, SHIFTING WEIGHT FROM SIDE TO SIDE OR STRETCHING THE HINDLEGS BACK BEHIND HIM.

The legs

Horses stomp their feet in much the same way toddlers (and even some so-called adults!) do when they are irritated. Foot-stomping may be triggered by flies, standing too long on the crossties or impatience at a delayed meal.

Foot-stomping is also the next step after ear-pinning, if the horse is being annoyed or angered. In those circumstances, foot-stomping is a clear warning: "Keep it up and my next move will be to bite, strike or kick." There is rarely need to reprimand a horse for occasionally pinning his ears. After all, he is entitled to his opinions. However, foot-stomping is a more blatant form of resistance or defiance if it occurs in reaction to something you are trying to do. **Do not ignore it or the horse may be encouraged to take a more aggressive stand.**

Pawing is one of the more irritating behaviors, bordering on nerve wracking. Pawing that begins as soon as you put the horse on crossties or start feeding or turnout procedures, probably comes from frustration, impatience or boredom rather than from aggression.

There are times, though, when pawing is a sign of aggression. This is usually seen when two horses are preparing to have a confrontation. The pawing will precede more serious aggression, such as biting or striking. A horse who paws when you work on him or attempt to perform some procedure such as paste deworming is also showing active resistance. (This behavior should be dealt with firmly and immediately, before the horse gets bolder.)

Body language of the sick or hurt horse

If there is one time when we most wish the horse could talk it is when something is wrong. How much easier it would be if the horse could have told us at noon that he had a mild bellyache rather than to find him at 4 p.m. writhing in pain. Maybe he did. You can pick up clues from your horse that will let you know early that something is wrong physically.

Abdominal pain/colic

The horse with mild abdominal pain may pick at his food, taking small mouthfuls and walking away, and play in the water without actually drinking. Complete loss of interest in these things develops as pain worsens. When resting in the stall, the horse may swish his tail, pin his ears slightly and often will shift weight from one hind leg to the other. You may even notice he isn't walking quite right in the hindquarters out in the pasture. With more severe pain, all of these signs become more obvious.

A partially dropped penis, without any attempt to urinate, is common. With worse pain, the animal may actually stretch out and assume the position for urination but will not urinate.

Breathing rate may be slightly elevated in early or mild colic/abdominal pain but will progress to obvious blowing as distress increases. Horses with mild abdominal pain may be found lying down quietly at times of the day when they would normally be expected to be up. If you encourage them to rise, they will often show you one or more of the other signs of mild abdominal pain if you watch them for a few minutes. As pain mounts, rolling or pawing may develop — often violently and insistently.

Breathing difficulties/chest pain

The horse with breathing difficulty will typically stand still, elbows slightly turned out, with head and neck dropped and slightly stretched forward. If you watch the movement of the chest as he breathes, you will see that breaths are shallow (chest barely moving) and more frequent.

Tying-up/founder

You may hear people say they can tell if a horse is tied-up or foundered, just by looking at him in his stall. In both cases, **the horse will often assume a rigid posture with muscles tensed and feet squarely planted.** The horse will also be reluctant to move/walk. These two conditions look so much alike that many, many people have misdiagnosed one for the other. However, the astute observer will examine the horse to differentiate the two.

The first thing you should do is feel the horse's feet. If they are red-hot or ice-cold, founder is likely. History is also important. If the horse was worked recently, tying-up is more likely.

With founder, the horse will stand with his hindlegs far underneath him in an attempt to shift all the weight to his hindquarters. The muscles appear bulging and tight because of the work they are doing. When you force the acutely foundered horse to move, his front feet will seem glued to the ground way out in front of him, and he will quiver with pain and blow hard every time a front foot hits the ground.

The tied-up horse, on the other hand, will avoid putting weight on his hindquarters, shifting weight from side to side or stretching the hindlegs back behind him. His feet will have a normal temperature, and he will take normal steps in front, with tiny, mincing steps or extreme stiffness behind. The tied-up horse will permit you to pick up a front foot if you are careful to keep it low to the ground and not shift weight to the hindquarters, while a foundered horse will not.

Lameness/sore leg

A horse with even nagging, low-grade leg pain will habitually rest the hurting leg when he's left alone. If a front leg is bothering him, he will often place it farther out in front of him when standing still or when bending down to graze or eat off the floor.

A horse with pain in his hoof, sesamoid bone, suspensory or tendon will put less weight on his heel than his toe. This can be detected even with both feet on the ground, since the tendons and ligaments of the sore leg will not be as prominent and tight as those of the other leg, which is bearing more weight.

Horses with hock pain will rest the most painful leg by placing it farther under the body and more toward the midline than the other leg. When they turn in their stalls they will often pivot on the hindlegs rather than picking them up and putting them down. If both hocks hurt, they may place both legs far forward and under the body, looking like they are about to "dog sit."

Stifle pain causes a horse to rest the painful joint by taking weight off the leg and standing with the stifle joint rotated slightly to the outside.

Nonspecific signs of trouble

Just like people, horses get grumpy if something is bothering them. **Behavior changes are the most common early signs of trouble.** A usually pleasant horse may pin his ears and swish his tail at routine tasks like grooming or saddling. When being worked, the horse may be less supple or frankly resistant about tasks that he anticipates will cause him pain. **Never dismiss this type of behavior as the horse being "sour" if he had previously been willing and cooperative.** Pay close attention to those movements that the horse is resisting, and they will often provide valuable clues for you, your farrier and your veterinarian.

A change in appetite is another hallmark that something is amiss. The healthy horse loves to eat. Horses who become picky or refuse their usual diet should be watched closely. When horses are on turnout, be alert for the horse who is slow to come to eat and/or isolates himself from the others. PH

11

Good Farrier Traits

*We want our horses to have great hooves.
After all, there's truth to the adage
"No hoof, no horse." But can we truly ensure that our
horses get good farrier care? Absolutely, because much
of the responsibility rests in the owner's hands.*

Considering that the average horseowner spends in excess of $300 per year per horse on hoof care, more than just the health and usefulness of a horse depends on good farrier care — the health of the owner's wallet does as well.

A good shoeing job starts with the farrier's complete evaluation of each horse as an individual. The farrier's initial examination will include noting how the horse travels, watching each leg to see if the horse swings it to the inside or the outside. He'll probably watch your horse move away and then toward him to see how each foot lands. **Normally, the foot should land level, which means both the inside and outside heel of the foot touch the ground at the same time.** Sometimes it may be necessary to have one side of the foot lower than the other to change the horse's way of going (corrective trimming) or to improve his comfort.

The farrier will watch to see if the horse has a tendency to strike one foot with the other. If there is a problem, such as forging, he'll watch to see if the horse does this naturally or only under saddle (forging is sometimes caused by the rider). He'll see if the horse reaches far enough forward or too far forward with his back legs.

On close examination, the farrier will likely assess the current hoof angles, determining whether any changes are in order, as well as how the horse has worn his shoes and general hoof health.

Finally, the farrier will talk to you about your use of the horse, how often you ride and where you turn him out. He may even ask about feed if he detects a problem that may be nutritionally related, such as shelly hooves. Discuss what you know of the horse's shoeing history, any problems, such as tripping frequently, as well as any concerns you have, regardless of how trivial they may seem.

Good and bad farrier traits

A good farrier is often also a top horseman, which is evident in the way he works with horses and how they respond to him. **Farriers who truly care about their clients will do what is necessary to make the horse comfortable.** We know of farriers who get down on their knees to trim tiny ponies and give geriatric horses breaks while trimming, because the farrier knows the infirmities of old age make it difficult to hold up one leg for any length of time. Knowledgeable farriers are likely to spot stifle problems and adjust the way they pick up back feet so the horse is most comfortable.

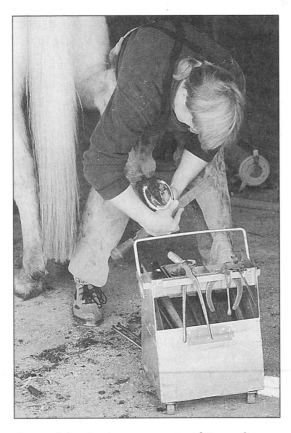

A good farrier is an expert at his craft, as well as a good horseman.

A good farrier uses the right nails for the right shoe and hoof. The slimmest nail to do the job is generally easiest on the hoof, but it must set properly in the shoe to hold it on. This is also why some farriers advise against resets. The shoe may look good, but it's entirely possible that the nail holes in the shoe are starting to wear and the nails will not lock in and hold the shoe secure. **A reset shoe may fall**

off a lot sooner than a new shoe. Sure, your horse will need to rewear his breakover point, but that's not a hardship for him.

Bad farriers are more interested in the number of horses they can do in a day than in the quality of their work. A good farrier will take the time that is necessary to do your horse correctly, and the time varies among farriers and with horses. A rush job will leave an uneven trim, improperly placed nails or nails that are scattered all over the hoof wall (you want nails placed all in a straight line or with two high and two low). Clinches should be tight and smooth. A bad farrier will leave them rough or too long, hoping they'll hold the shoe longer. If that shoe does come off, it's likely to take most of the hoof wall with it.

Corrective and therapeutic work

While the farrier can change the shape of almost any hoof, it isn't always in the best interest of the horse. Corrective work should be done at as early an age as possible, before the horse has matured and the bones are set in place, usually at less than five years of age. **Making corrective changes in hoof shape and angles can put excessive strain and stress on older tendons and ligaments, which can result in other, more serious problems.**

If corrective work is determined to be a benefit to your horse, it should be done gradually. You'll have to expect to have your farrier back more frequently than the normal six- to eight-week interval. This is the same for therapeutic work, such as for a foundered horse or one with navicular disease. Regular preventative care is your best bet.

Generally speaking, the angle of the hoof should match the angle of the pastern, which often mirrors the angle of the horse's shoulder.

Hot or cold

The decision on whether to hot-shoe (heat the shoe in a forge) or cold-shoe a horse is a decision between farrier and owner. If clips (the sides of the shoe drawn up to help hold the shoe on) are necessary, the farrier is likely to hot-shoe the horse. Hot shoeing helps seat the clips into the hoof wall; however, the farrier can also nip out a small space on the side of the hoof for the clips and put the shoes on after they cool off.

Most horses are cold shod with keg shoes. Keg shoes are manufactured and then shaped on the anvil by the farrier to fit the horse's hoof. Many farriers also hand-make shoes from steel bar stock, but you can expect to pay top dollar for this time-consuming and labor-intensive job. For most horses, hand-made shoes offer no advantages over keg shoes.

Lameness and the farrier

One of the most frustrating phone calls for a farrier to receive is that a horse is lame and would he please come out and look at it. While lamenesses certainly do occur in the hoof, the farrier is limited in what he can do.

If the lameness occurred without any other probable cause within 24 hours of a shoeing, it is possible that the cause is a "hot" nail,

which means the nail was placed too close to the edge of the white line and is causing the horse pain. However, this problem is rare with a good farrier and will be seen quickly, sometimes within a few hours of the shoeing. **A hot nail is not likely to cause a lameness a week later.**

A thoughtful farrier will hold the horse's foot at a height comfortable for the horse, as well as being workable for himself.

The farrier can also help with lamenesses due to bruises and most abscesses, although some abscesses are deep enough to warrant the help of the vet and some penicillin. If the farrier recommends you call the vet and then report back to him, do so. He's recommending what he thinks is best for your horse, and the fact that he wants to know how it turned out shows he's concerned.

If your description of the horse's symptoms does make him think the lameness may be hoof-related and agrees to come out, don't expect him to appear and not get paid because "he didn't do anything." He arrived, shared his expertise and advised you on your best course of action, even if that was to call the veterinarian.

Good hoof care steps

■ *Clean stalls daily.*

■ *Pick and inspect hooves daily.*

■ *Maintain proper nutrition, especially biotin and vitamin E, supplementing if necessary.*

■ *Minimize mud holes in fields and around water troughs.*

■ *Pick up rocks, sticks and other debris in your paddocks and pastures that can cause punctures and chipping.*

■ *Minimize the use of hoof moisturizers, unless advised otherwise by your farrier.*

■ *Stay current in hoof care with regular farrier visits every six to eight weeks all year-round.*

■ *Try to avoid riding on asphalt and rocky areas.*

Customer responsibilities

■ Regardless of your farrier's skill, he can't nail to or trim a moving target. If your horse won't stand and behave, you aren't likely to get a good job. It's up to the owner to teach the horse to stand still for the farrier. Many farriers won't even deal with a difficult horse. **It's simply not worth the money or risk of injury, which can put them out of income for many months.**

Asking your farrier to correct your horse isn't fair. While he may want to give that horse a strong whack, it isn't his place. Not only do all horsemen have different levels of acceptable forms of discipline, a single whack each time the farrier arrives will only cause your horse to resent the visits. Work with the unwilling horse daily to train him to stand still. Don't just pick out his hooves; brush them out too. Hold his legs up for a few minutes, imitating the time it takes to trim a hoof. **A horse commonly will stand better for the familiar person than for the new person, the farrier. So you'll have to train him beyond where the horse just barely stands still for handling of his feet.**

■ Be on time for your appointments. That means have the horse in the barn, cleaned up and ready when the farrier arrives. Good farriers try to arrive on time. It's usually something beyond his control, like owners having to catch their horses, that caused him to run late in the first place.

This is another reason why scheduling is so important. Don't expect your farrier to just automatically throw in another horse during his visit. Farriers schedule appointments based on the number of horses and type of work they need to do at each barn. One extra horse can put a shoer an hour or more behind for the entire day.

■ While problems can arise for both horseowners and farriers, it's annoying to receive a call the night before that the appointment is canceled without a valid reason. Of course, that's not as bad as arriving at a barn to find no one around. Most farriers will not work on a horse without someone present, not only to pay the bill, but also to help in the event of an emergency or to answer questions. And if no one is at the barn, they assume they've been stood up.

■ Call to schedule an appointment a reasonable time before the horse needs shoeing. We guarantee your farrier wants you to know that your "emergency" is not his emergency when your horse is already three weeks overdue. You can't expect him to simply squeeze you in because you forgot to make your regular appointment.

■ Have your horse trimmed regularly. **If you let your horse go too long between shoeings because the hoof still "looks good," you're asking for trouble.** It can cause soreness or excessive growth with long toes and low-heel problems. If your farrier suggests you need to do your horse more frequently, this suggestion is made for the good of your horse.

The hoof on the left belongs to a horse who doesn't ordinarily wear shoes. It is well trimmed. The hoof on the right is the result of not being trimmed on time. The hoof is broken up so much that it would be difficult to shoe.

■ Keep the area where the farrier works well lit and uncluttered. Dirty, poorly lit aisles with brooms and muck baskets all over the place are unsafe for horse, farrier and handler. Keep commotion to a minimum in the area where the horse is being shod or trimmed.

■ When the farrier is there, pay attention to what's going on with your horse, not to the other horses or people in the barn. Stand where the farrier directs and discipline your horse. Avoid running to answer the phone (use an answering machine). Some farriers allow horses to be tied while they work on them, but others don't. While this is a matter of preference, we all know that tying a horse is not the safest way to work on him.

■ Don't impose on your farrier by asking him to do things beyond his specialty, such as advising you about training matters or vaccinating your horse.

■ If your horse loses a shoe, avoid shopping around for the "first available" farrier. In fairness, you should call your own farrier and find out what his schedule is like. Unless your horse is grossly overdue, most farriers will consider a lost shoe somewhat of an emergency and try to get there within 24 hours. While you wait for your farrier to arrive, protect the hoof wall from further damage with duct tape and Vetrap.

What to look for

A well-trimmed hoof is rounded and has no sharp edges. When you look at the outside of the hoof wall, you shouldn't see rasp marks that go beyond the bottom third of the hoof. The hoof wall rests evenly on the ground.

When you pick up the hoof, the bottom should look balanced and symmetrical. You'll note that the farrier has cut away excess sole.

The heels should be even, so the horse lands properly. Heels that are too narrow can cause contracted heels. The excess frog is trimmed away — no ragged edges — and the frog should be dry and spongy, just as you'd expect a "shock absorber" to be.

The hoof angle should closely match the natural angle of your horse's pastern. A lower angle is often used on racehorses to increase their stride, while higher angles often indicate an attempt to compensate for a chronic lameness, such as one due to navicular disease. Back hooves naturally have a slightly higher angle than front ones.

A poorly shod hoof won't be pretty. It may be uneven and look bull-nosed. You shouldn't see gaps of shoe extended beyond the hoof wall nor should you see hoof farther beyond the edge of the shoe. The heel of the shoe should set a little farther out than the hoof to allow for proper expansion and contraction of the heel. Some farriers try to fit the hoof into a smaller shoe to save time; don't let them. Not only is this uncomfortable and unfair to your horse, it can cause problems down the road.

What your farrier hates

- *People who cancel at the last minute or don't show up*

- *Bad lighting in the work area*

- *Cluttered work areas*

- *Unnecessary commotion in the work area*

- *Interruptions because the handler has to answer the phone, check on the help, dog, etc.*

- *Handlers who don't pay attention*

- *Calling for the farrier when the horse is lame (that's usually the vet's job)*

- *Expecting the farrier to drop everything and get to your barn tomorrow*

- *Unruly horses with owners who do not discipline and teach the horses to stand*

- *Expecting the farrier to discipline the horse and teach him to stand*

- *Bad pays and bounced checks*

Care of your shoeing dollar

Hire the best farrier you can get. In most areas anyone can call himself a horseshoer, so ask for recommendations from veterinarians and knowledgeable horsepeople. Most farriers are professional, but every area has a local ne'er-do-well who puts shoes on horses for quick money. As with other services, you get what you pay for. Although a top farrier may be more expensive, your horses and peace of mind are worth the cost.

Discuss fees in advance of the farrier doing the work. While there are exceptions, most farriers set what they feel are fair fees to cover their expenses, plus profit for their labor. They too must pay self-employment taxes, health insurance, truck payments and so on.

Stretching the time between farrier visits is a classic example of "penny wise and pound foolish." **Trimming the hoof every six to eight weeks is the optimum time frame for proper hoof care.** Keeping to this will save you money in the long run, preventing veterinary bills and down time for the horse.

The farrier can do many things to customize your horse's shoes, but the fact is the simpler, the better. If your horse doesn't need bar shoes, egg bar shoes, clips, trailers or pads, don't bother. If steel shoes will work for your discipline, there's no reason to pay more for aluminum shoes, glue-on shoes or special shock-absorbing shoes.

As one farrier once told an over-enthusiastic customer who was scanning the shoes in the truck for her horse, "This isn't a shoe store." It's a collection of horseshoes to fit a variety of horses, and you're lucky if your horse just needs a simple, basic steel shoe.

The value of farrier-certifying organizations

Any one of the three national organizations we list here can give you the names of qualified farriers in your area. While there's a lot of squabbling among farriers and among associations as to which is the best organization and the value of certification overall, the truth is that many top farriers never bother with any certification due to the politics involved in these groups. They are, however, likely to be a member of one or more of these organization in order to receive educational materials.

American Farriers Association
4059 Iron Works Pkwy, Suite 2, Lexington, KY 40511
606-233-7411
www.amfarriers.com

Brotherhood of Working Farriers Association
14013 East Hwy. 136, LaFayette, GA 30728
706-397-8047
www.bwfa.net PH

Our thanks to contributing writer Lee Foley

12

Cribbing Is Complicated

*Not to be confused with wood-chewing
or air-swallowing, cribbing is a destructive vice
that truly feels "good" to the horse.*

M uch has been written about cribbing — most of it spec-
ulation. Cribbing has been called everything from a stable vice to a nervous habit to an obsessive-compulsive
disorder. The fact is, we really don't completely understand cribbing, since it is impossible to ask the horse what he
feels when cribbing, what it does for his state of mind or to otherwise do any psychoanalytical evaluation!

Cribbing is a peculiar and characteristic behavior. The horse will
grasp the edge of an object — such as a stall door or a ledge in his
stall or a fence rail — firmly between his teeth. He then appears to
arch his neck and flex his neck and throat muscles. Inside his mouth,
he moves his tongue and throat as if swallowing, as he begins to
suck in, much as if he were drinking a milkshake through a straw,
but with his jaw, throat and neck rigidly fixed. This allows the upper
part of the esophagus (the tube between throat and stomach) to bal-
loon up as a large amount of air rushes into the upper esophagus,
causing a characteristic grunt-like noise.

The horse holds this position, then the air gets released back into
his throat/mouth area. When horses are cribbing, they appear to be
totally involved in what they are doing. Many horses crib in a rhythmic pattern, "resting" for brief periods before repeating the cycle.

One thing that seems clear is cribbing is different from other bad
habits or vices, like pawing, wood-chewing (actually wood-eating),
stall-walking or weaving. These latter types of behavior are clearly

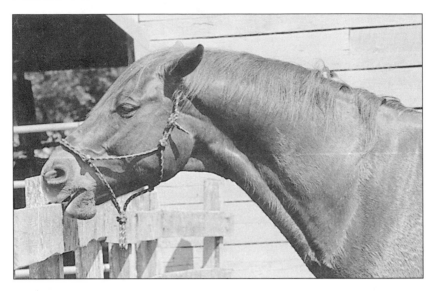

This experienced cribber will crib the moment his collar is removed. Note the flexion of his neck muscles and his total pre-occupation with what he is doing. Confirmed cribbers don't need much to grasp. In fact, while some put their teeth around some-thing — like a pipe rail in a pipe corral — most just brace against the edge of a fence or bucket.

associated with either stress or boredom; they're more common both in horses who don't have enough exercise and in those who are very fit but confined to a stall except for relatively brief exercise periods during the day (i.e., racehorses). Cribbing isn't like that. It is not as common as those other behavior patterns, and it often does not respond to such things as giving the horse more roughage/hay to amuse himself with or even to a switch from stall confinement to turnout.

Horses who paw, weave or stall-walk are usually clearly agitated and worked up while doing it. Their movement is a physical manifestation of frustration at confinement. The human equivalent would be something like foot-shaking, floor-walking, finger-tapping, nail-biting or hair-twirling — physical signs of anxiety but not effective in relieving it.

Wood-chewing is more associated with boredom — the equine equivalent of human compulsive eating. Most horses will stop chewing wood as soon as you throw them a flake of hay. (Though, there are some "equine termites" who just can't seem to resist boring through every piece of available wood.)

Cribbing is more complicated. **Studies have shown that cribbing has a soothing effect on the horse — his heart rate actually slows while he cribs.** The horse cribs to get a "high," and the behavior becomes firmly ingrained by the pleasure the horse gets from it — like when laboratory mice learn to drink water "spiked" with alcohol or a pleasurable drug. This would explain why many cribbers go to great lengths to crib, despite everything the owner does to prevent it. **The best description of cribbing is that it is a form of self-stimulation.**

Cribbing and endorphins

Produced by the body, endorphins are potent narcotic-like chemicals that cause a sense of well being. They are responsible for what is called the "runner's high" in people. Endorphins have also been proven to increase with heavy training in horses. Studies in Germany have shown that cribbers have endorphin levels that are eight times higher than in noncribbers!

However, endorphin levels do not change immediately after cribbing. Studies in Scotland with cribbers showed that giving them the drug Naloxone, which blocks the effects of narcotics, significantly reduced cribbing. (Cribbers in that study spent more time resting, instead.) Because the endorphin levels in the German horses did not jump as a direct result of cribbing, those researchers theorized the high endorphin levels were caused by general stress. However, the blood levels of the stress hormone cortisol were not any higher in the cribbers than the noncribbers. Bottom line is there is indeed a connection between the cribbing and endorphin levels. This suggests that cribbing might be more like an addiction than a simple habit.

Cribbing surgery

You may have heard of surgery to stop cribbing. There actually is such a procedure, although many reputable veterinarians refuse to do it. The surgery involves cutting muscles in the horse's throat/neck, thus making it impossible to set his head in that odd, rigid way required to crib. This will stop the horse from making the grunting noise, but it won't stop him from trying to crib, and the underlying causes, whatever they may be, will still be there. Cribbing surgery also disfigures the horse (to varying degrees, depending on which procedure is used) and isn't 100 percent successful. **We do not recommend cribbing surgery.**

Cribbers don't swallow air

For years it was thought that cribbers were swallowing air, which could lead to abdominal discomfort. Some insurance companies won't insure cribbers for this reason. However, studies using fluoroscopy (X-ray cameras that allow you to see what is happening inside the horse) and endoscopes (that watch the interior of the horse's throat while he is cribbing) show that horses actually swallow little air, if any, so these fears are unfounded. Although it was once thought that cribbing was responsible for colic, flatulence and poor digestion, it is now generally accepted that cribbing doesn't cause these problems in most horses, and correction of the habit will not alleviate such symptoms.

Though he's not trying to eat the wood, a cribber can still damage fence and barn surfaces.

So, does that mean that cribbing is OK? Cribbing, per se, does not have a direct negative impact on the horse's health. But it is responsible for possible premature wearing of the teeth, damage to biting surfaces, and hypertrophy of the sternocephalicus muscle (the large muscle on the undersurface of the neck), which not only looks ugly but can interfere with some performances. The behavior is classified as a vice because owners consider it an undesirable activity, and cribbing often has a distinctly negative impact on the environment in which the cribber lives (the barn looks gnawed on, and in some cases, the horse pulls hard enough that he pulls buckets or boards off the stall wall).

Stopping the diehard cribber

The hard-core cribber will crib in his stall or out in the pasture, often without obvious sources of "stress" that might contribute to this behavior. If cribbing straps don't work, you will need to do some stall remodeling. The interior of the stall must have no protruding edges. Even a lip that is too small to actually let the horse crib will be a temptation. Use wire mesh set flush with the inside-edge wood or bars that are very narrowly spaced. Use a full door or a door that is half-screen/mesh and will close flush with the lower half.

If the horse tries to crib on buckets, remove the feed tube as soon as he is finished and build a special holder for the water bucket. The bucket should sit two to three inches down inside a wooden protector. A suitable design would be an upper flat surface at least six inches wide (i.e., too wide for the horse to get his mouth around it) with sides that are wider at the bottom than the top (if sides of the "box" slope in toward the wall the horse will try to get a grip on them with his teeth). You may have to water more often, but the horse won't be able to crib.

Outside, your best protection against cribbing on fences is an electric "shocker" wire. This must be set far enough away from the actual fence line and toward the horse so the horse cannot stretch his head past the wire to grab the fence on the other side. Run the hot wire flush with the top of the fence. If the horse tries to crib lower on the fence posts, rails or planks, you may have to run another hot wire at that level also or use heavy mesh mounted on the inside (toward the pasture) of the fencing.

The simplest way to limit a horse from cribbing is with a cribbing strap, a leather or leather-and-metal device fastened around the horse's neck/throat area to prevent the movements necessary to swallow air. **To be effective, the strap must be tight enough to restrict motion in the throat area, but not so tight as to**

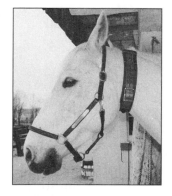

This classic, simple cribbing strap is a 2.5-inch-wide strip of harness leather that fastens behind the horse's ears, high on the neck/throat area. This collar was made by Weaver Leather (800-693-2837/330-674-1782).

cause discomfort. A correctly fitted strap allows the horse to eat and drink freely but not to crib.

Begin by tightening the strap enough that it can't turn around on the horse's neck. Continue tightening until the horse is unable to crib. A closely trimmed bridle path makes adjustment easier. Even with an optimal fit, most cribbing straps cause rubbing and hair loss over time, but it is made worse if the collar is too tight or too loose. Fleece padding and frequent checks on the health of the skin and coat under the strap, can minimize this problem.

Is cribbing contagious?

Many people don't want a cribber in their barn for fear that the other horses will pick up this bad habit. Studies of barns/farms that have cribbers, however, usually show that only a few (maybe even just one or two) of the horses crib, although other bad habits/vices may be evident in the other horses.

Some foals of mares who crib develop the habit. It may be more likely for the foal of a cribber to begin than another adult horse in the vicinity, although we could not find good statistics to prove this. The foal is more likely to imitate his dam, or perhaps has inherited the genetic and chemical make-up that makes this activity especially pleasurable.

So cribbing is not contagious, per se, and because a horse is stalled next to a cribber doesn't mean that the horse will begin cribbing. Some barns are stressful places, however, and when a horse lives without adequate turnout, pleasant surroundings and regular exercise, grooming and feeding times, etc., he's more likely to look for stress-relieving behaviors. **PH**

13

Open Knees

*You have probably heard someone say
a horse's knees were "still open" and you knew
it meant he has not finished growing. But how
can you tell if he's mature enough to start riding?*

Each year countless folks wait patiently for their mare to foal. Then they wait patiently through the first two years of feeding and caring for their young horse, looking forward to riding him for years to come. But along about the second or third year of his life, they get impatient because the horse looks big and strong enough to carry them. They begin his riding training, not realizing they could cause irreversible damage. Let's look at how bone forms and when it's safe to ride your young horse.

Anyone who has handled a foal's legs knows how light they are. That's because, like bird bones, there's not much bone weight, for their size. As the bone matures, little islands of bone-forming cells, called "centers of ossification" (ossification is the process of hardening, calcifying and turning into bone), appear

This well-bred young horse has a bright future, if he isn't worked too hard too soon. Chronic back problems and ill-defined gait difficulties, as well as lamenesses, may be avoided if these bones are not stressed too early.

throughout the bones. **Ossification spreads outward from these centers until the entire bone, except areas of the growth plates and the ends of the bones, has calcium and other minerals in it.** As the bone ossifies, it gets thicker and heavier.

So, how does the bone grow longer and the horse taller? At each end of the bone, just before the flare, is a growth plate (physis), like little plates sitting on top and at the bottom of a long tube (the bone). At the top and bottom edges of each plate, the connective-tissue cells change character, becoming bone cells. (The area of bone cells that is produced on the "far" end of the physis is called the epiphysis.) There are only cartilage cells at the end of the bones, not in the growth plate.

As long as that growth plate continues to produce connective-tissue cells at a faster rate than they become converted into bone cells and are calcified, the bone will continue to grow in length. **Once the bone on top of the growth plate grows to meet the bone below the growth plate, the growth plate disappears, and the joint closes.**

When growth plates close

Hash marks (where the bones flare) indicate the growth plates in the ankle.

So, when people refer to a horse's knees as being "open" or "closed," they are talking about that region of the bone called the growth plate. Simply put, "open" means the bone is still growing, and "closed" that it has stopped growing in length.

The radius is the long bone running down from the horse's elbow to his knee (the same bone that goes from your elbow to your wrist). The growth plate we usually refer to is in the distal part of the radius (closest to the ground), about 1½ to 2 inches above the top of the knee joint, in the "waist" of bone just above the prominent ends that form the surface of the upper knee joint. If you run your hand down the horse's leg along the anterior (front) surface, you can clearly feel the edges of the bone and how it flares out into a wider surface just before ending at the top of the knee.

People focus on the knee because this growth plate closes later than the others, becoming fused at about 3½ years in most horses. Only the bones of the spine close later (at about four to five years).

Actual growth plate closing times

As you might expect, there are many growth plates located throughout the horse's skeleton. The radius also has a growth plate at the proximal (closer to the body) end, which closes at 15 to 18 months. A smaller bone runs beside it, the ulna. The proximal/upper ulna closes at about 3½ years, and the distal portion at a variable time. The humerus, located between shoulder and elbow, also has two growth plates (closing at 3½ years for the proximal and 15 to 18 months for the distal physis). The pelvis reaches its final size in 10 to 12 months, while the bones of the back leg follow roughly the same time course as those of the front leg.

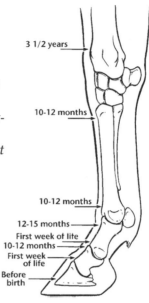

3 1/2 years

10-12 months

10-12 months

12-15 months

First week of life

10-12 months

First week of life

Before birth

If potential damage to the legs is not enough to dissuade you from waiting to start that young horse, consider that the bones of his spine are not completely formed/fused until the age of four or five.

Determining if growth plates are closed or open

It is sometimes possible to see the area of the epiphysis and physis in the region of the knee. These knees are often referred to as "boxy." The bone is prominent in the lower portion of the radius, just above the knee. However, this boxy appearance does not necessarily mean the growth plates are still open. Many horses, especially large-boned types and/or larger breeds, have boxy-appearing joints well into their fourth or fifth year (sometimes indefinitely). The fact is there is no way to determine if growth plates are open or closed simply by looking at, or feeling, a horse's knee. X-rays are necessary.

This horse had a promising career as a jumper, but he was started on big fences too early. The result was a growth-plate injury, which led to this knee deformity. The horse is permanently unsound.

On X-rays, bone shows up as white, and the physis looks like a fracture — a dark line through the bone — because there is no bone in the region. As bone growth slows, the growth plate becomes more and more dense until it cannot be distinguished from the rest of the bone on an X-ray. This is a fairly accurate way to determine if a bone has stopped growing, but it is not foolproof.

Microscopic study of bone from young horses has shown that complete closure may not occur for several months after they appear closed on X-rays. What this means is that there is still a tiny zone of cartilage or incompletely ossified bone cells in the region of the growth plate. This is important to know when deciding upon a training/exercise schedule for the horse.

Training the growing horse

Exercise is beneficial to growing animals, resulting in stronger bones and joints. However, it must be done in moderation because:

■ The bones are not as structurally strong as in an adult horse.

■ The layers of cartilage in the joints are not as thick or strong and can be crushed or deformed.

■ There are many more blood vessels in the growing sections of bone in a young horse, and excessive pressure can shut these down or cause inflammation, making the bone begin to grow unevenly.

The growth plate is a "weak spot" in the bone. Because it is not mineralized, it is not as rigid and strong as regular bone. In extreme cases a bone can fracture through the physis. Some people call this a "slipped growth plate," because X-rays show the epiphysis sitting off to one side.

Because you can injure immature bones and joints, moderation should be the rule when working and training young horses. **There is no doubt that horses who are turned out in large areas or worked**

lightly before the age of four or five have longer useful lives with fewer bone and joint problems than horses put to work at earlier ages. However, few people wait four or five years to begin working their young stock. In their favor is the research evidence that shows clear benefit in terms of stronger bone (for the age group) when young animals have regular, moderate exercise. The question becomes what exactly constitutes "moderate" exercise.

We can narrow the range of safe activities by starting with things that definitely should be avoided: jumping, extreme speed, cutting (or any activity that involves sharp turns, especially at speed) and any work that calls for weight to be shifted in an abnormal manner (sliding stops, pulling heavy weights) onto the front or back legs. Although you may get away with these maneuvers without your young horse going lame, the damaging consequences of this could appear years down the road.

THE FACT IS THERE IS NO WAY

TO DETERMINE IF GROWTH PLATES ARE

OPEN OR CLOSED SIMPLY BY LOOKING AT,

OR FEELING, A HORSE'S KNEE.

X-RAYS ARE NECESSARY.

For example, veterinarians are just now realizing that tiny chip fractures off the front of the pastern (in the ankle) or in other joints are probably the result of injury to the bone that occurred at a young age. When the bone formed following this insult, it was not as strong and probably not properly aligned with the rest of the bone. The result is a chipping off of the weaker bone sometime later.

Evidence is also growing that osteochondrosis dessicans, a serious developmental abnormality of joint cartilage, may be caused at least in part by excessive stress on the developing joint cartilage and the underlying, growing bone.

Conformation also should be considered when designing an exercise program for the growing horse. Any conformation abnormality (and virtually any horse will have less-than-perfect legs, even if it is only during a temporary growth phase) causes weight to be distributed unevenly, and this means that even less force may produce an injury.

Let's use the front leg as an example. If a horse has perfect conformation, you could stand directly in front of him and draw a line from the middle of the bone above the knee, down through the middle of the knee, cannon bone, ankle, pastern and foot and hit the ground in the exact middle of the toe. With this alignment of the bones, forces are absorbed equally by the center, outside and inside of the bones and the joints. However, conformation imperfections, such as cannon bones set more to the outside of the knee or legs that point outward from the knee down, change the weight distribution.

This uneven distribution can crush delicate blood vessels and cartilage, damaging the forming tissue. If the weight imbalance is not quite as severe, the result can be the opposite; the developing bone receives signals that it must be stronger on one side than the other and it compensates by growing at an accelerated rate on the overstressed side. **This is why even slight problems, such as a little toeing-in or toeing-out in a young horse, can turn into a more exaggerated problem if measures are not taken to correct any possible causes.**

Finally, to avoid damaging bone or creating crooked legs, it is imperative that a young horse be correctly trimmed before and at all steps during a formal exercise program. **Trimming has much more dramatic effects on a young horse than on one that is fully formed — both for better and for worse.**

So, what does this tell us if we participate in a sport requiring young horses to compete at an early age? It says that we do put them at risk for lamenesses and arthritis years down the

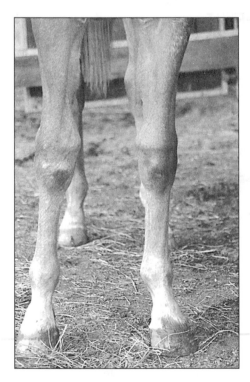

The boxy appearance of this horse's knees does not necessarily mean that the growth plates are still open.

road. It implies that if we are willing to assume that risk, we have to give the horse every advantage to grow solid bones. This would include careful attention to feeding, making sure the horse has adequate mineral balance in his feed as well as protein.

For any young horse, whether we work him or not, we should minimize his stopping, turning and jamming-into-the-ground. This includes teaching him to stand tied without pulling back, so we don't risk injury to neck bones, and sacking-out and spook-in-place work so he doesn't injure himself if he gets frightened. Finally, if it's not necessary to ask your horse to carry weight or jump at an early age, don't do it. The same holds true for excessive lungeing or riding in small circles. There's so much you can teach your horse before you ride him that will make him a better riding horse; your time with him may be better spent doing those things.

A few words about epiphysitis

No discussion of growth plates and growing bones would be complete without mentioning epiphysitis. The condition is really an inflammation of the physis (growth plate), not the epiphysis, but because the swelling is located low on the growing bone it is often called epiphysitis.

*Epiphysitis may involve any bone, but the lower growth plates, and occasionally the knee, are most often involved. **A horse with epiphysitis will have heat, swelling and tenderness at the distal ends of the bone, with some degree of lameness.** The exact cause of epiphysitis is not well understood. It seems to be most common in horses that are growing rapidly, have been weaned and are on hard ground, such as during the summer.*

*It was once thought that excess protein in the diet causes epiphysitis, but this has proven to be incorrect. **In fact, growing bone requires not only a high-protein intake (16% to 18% protein diet) but high-quality protein (i.e. alfalfa, milk-based supplements).** Although overfeeding/rapid growth/nutrition may play a role in epiphysitis, it has been impossible so far to identify any one factor, or even group of factors, that will put the horse at high risk of epiphysitis.*

It appears that epiphysitis is a result of a combination of factors — rapid growth, increasing body weight, unyielding ground surfaces that increase concussion, perhaps conformation faults and perhaps periods of heavier-than-normal exercise — all working together. The good news about epiphysitis is that most horses recover with no particular treatment and with no permanent consequences.

Current recommendations for managing horses with epiphysitis include feeding an adequate but not excessive diet (i.e., no attempts at "fattening"), judicious use of anti-inflammatory agents to make the horse comfortable and to speed resolution of the inflammation, and confinement to a relatively small pen/yard or a large roomy stall with generous, soft footing/bedding. You should avoid putting the horse with other animals when confrontations and rough housing will be likely. More aggressive measures such as hosing, icing and bandaging would also help but may not be practical with the young animal. Most cases resolve spontaneously in a few weeks with the above management. **PH**

14

Getting Back Into Shape

*You are itching to get back in the saddle again.
But what's your plan for getting your horse
and yourself back into riding condition?*

T he result of launching out on a ride physically unprepared is that a horse or rider, or both, may end up with the aches and pains from overdoing it, perhaps even a sprain or other injury that may put riding on hold again. To avoid injury, take time to make the first ride after a layoff as enjoyable and problem-free as possible.

Equipment check-out

Tack not used for weeks or months probably needs attention. Check your bridle, girths, reins and other equipment for drying, cracking or fraying. Stitching is prone to weakening or rotting in storage. Stiff, dry leather can often be rejuvenated by a thorough cleaning with saddle soap followed by several applications of neatsfoot oil or other conditioner prepared for leather. But, if you find your tack is brittle or has little tears in it, don't take chances: Replace it!

The condition of the saddle is especially important (to your horse's back!). If the saddle doesn't flex properly or if the padding has hardened, take it to a repair shop. Also replace corroded bits, metal rings and other metal connectors.

Pay special attention to saddle pads or blankets. Your horse's back will need some time to strengthen and toughen up. Irritation in the saddle area is more likely after a layoff, and it can cause the

"Who me — go back to work?" Sometimes reconditioning our horse to respond to our cues is as important as conditioning his body.

horse to stiffen his back muscles and become sore. An extra layer of padding next to the skin is a must for horses with histories of sore backs and a plus for any horse starting back in work.

When you check saddle fit, keep in mind that, like you if you haven't been exercising, your horse has probably changed dimensions. The saddle that fit him perfectly when he was in condition may not fit well when he's out of shape. If he's lost muscle mass, his withers may be more prominent, and additional padding may be necessary to make up the deficit. If he gained weight, padding under the saddle may make the saddle too tight. Check saddle fit periodically as the horse gains condition, because his body will continue to change shape.

Horse check-out

Give your horse a thorough grooming, noting any areas of heat or swelling, bumps, bites or skin problems. Then watch how he moves. Ask someone to jog the horse in hand or observe him on a lunge line to make sure he is sound.

Check up on routine health-maintenance procedures. Deworming and vaccinations should be done two to three weeks before resuming work. You can also ask the veterinarian to give your horse a quick going over to make sure you have not missed anything and to evaluate the status of any areas that caused problems in the past.

Hooves

Getting those hooves in condition to withstand regular work is also something you need to take care of before beginning your program. Horses who are accustomed to being barefoot may only need a little sprucing up. Those who have only had their shoes pulled for turnout may require shoeing again before you start. A horse's history is the best indicator of whether or not he needs shoes. If he needed them before lay-off, shoe him early instead of waiting for problems to develop. There are few things more frustrating for you or the horse than his being sidelined by sore feet.

The horse's diet

In the early stages of getting a horse back in shape, his basic diet may not need to change much, at least in terms of the amount of feed. If he is too heavy, don't necessarily cut his food but just start him exercising as we describe. The exercise alone will probably help him drop those few extra pounds. If the horse is too thin, begin gradually increasing his feed several weeks before riding begins. Add (or increase) grain and make sure parasites are not the problem. A dental check-up is also important.

High-quality protein is important to the exercising horse. **If the horse is receiving good alfalfa hay and/or has liberal access to young, good-quality pastures, an 8% or 10% protein grain will be adequate.** If you are feeding grass hay, however, you will need at least 12% protein feed for the exercising horse.

If the grain intake is minimal (less than 1/3 of

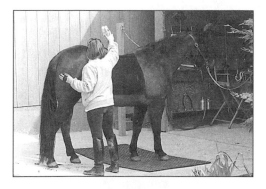

Vigorous grooming will help your horse shed his winter coat and you to get in shape.

total combined weight of hay and grain), use of a protein supplement might be advisable. We like Calf Manna (a half pound once a
day to start, gradually increasing to a half pound twice a day) as a
well-balanced, high-quality and economical protein supplement. It
also has liberal amounts of vitamin A, severely lacking in most grass
hays. (NOTE: Some horses are intolerant of the soybean protein in
this and other products. Problems include bloating, excessive gas
and possibly some diarrhea. Cutting back the amount and increasing it gradually usually solves the problem. If not, you will need to
meet protein needs by other dietary adjustments.)

The horse just beginning an exercise program probably does not
have any fancy vitamin and mineral needs, assuming that work is
resumed in a sane way. Use of a good, balanced multiple vitamin-
and-mineral supplement should be all you need to cover any increased needs. Any other supplements should be based on particular
problems your horse may have (i.e., antioxidants, vitamin E and se-
lenium for horses prone to tying-up or muscle soreness).

The conditioning program

*We tend to think of horses as natural athletes, and to a
certain extent this is true. Many factors enter into determining how much work a horse can safely do without
becoming sore or injured, including his age, the health of
his lungs, his body weight, lameness problems, foot
health and, in general, his athleticism and overall fitness.*
***We need to be especially careful when beginning a con-
ditioning program because the horse cannot tell us if he
feels stiff the next day or if a joint is aching a little.***
*Allowing this to happen, however, can easily lead to
lameness, behavior problems or resistance to our cues. It
is far easier to step up the pace of an exercise program if
the horse is handling it easily than it is to repair damage
done by going too quickly.*

*A good approach is to do the first few days to a week of
exercise together, with the rider on foot. This allows you
to quickly assess both how fit you are and how well the
horse is tolerating the work. This approach is especially
good when dealing with older horses who tend to lose
condition easily, with horses who have been out of work
for a prolonged time (more than a month) and for horses*

Brisk hand-walking, especially up and down hills, gets both horse and handler in shape. If you saddle the horse, his back will start to condition as well.

who were never used heavily even when they were last in work. We know from human sports medicine that walking at a brisk pace is just as beneficial in terms of burning calories as is jogging, improving muscle tone and improving cardiovascular efficiency, so let's begin there.

For Day One, tack up your horse as usual, but set out on a walk together. If you are sure your horse is in better shape than you are, pick your distances to match your condition (we don't want any stiff, sore or injured riders either!). One-and-a-half to two miles at a brisk walk over flat ground is a reasonable place to start.

If you pale at the thought of walking that far, you definitely will benefit from the exercise. You may also be surprised to see your horse's condition. A horse who is well conditioned for virtually any activity or sport should be able to cover this distance at this pace without turning a hair. On a pleasant day, there should be no sweating or obvious change in breathing pattern. When you notice your horse is carrying his head lower, breathing harder and faster and starting to break a sweat, you will know you have reached a level of exercise that is beyond his current fitness. (Note: These are general guidelines. There are other more sophisticated and more accurate methods of assessing fitness. However, for the purposes of this gradual reintroduction to exercise, these monitors of "stress" are both safe and effective.)

If both you and the horse tolerate Day One without a problem, increase distances by about a half-mile a day, until you are up to and comfortable at four to 4.5 miles. It is more than likely, however, that one or both of you will feel the effects of even this mild exercise.

If you tuckered out long before the horse, set the two-mile walk as your goal, but increase the horse's mileage as above, riding him at the end of your first mile and for the rest of the horse's extra mileage, then hand-walking him your last mile home. **Build up to a total of two miles for yourself gradually, in amounts that are comfortable to you, doing the same for the horse.** By the time you can easily walk the two miles, the horse may be up to four or more miles at the walk on flat ground. That's OK, though; we never really expected you to match or exceed your horse's tolerance for exercise. After all, this is why man needed horses in the first place!

Once you and your horse have comfortably gone through the walking-on-the-flat program, a good way to gain extra cardiovascular fitness and to condition the muscles, tendons and ligaments while avoiding injury is to progress to work on hills. But we don't mean Mt. Everest! An incline of as little as 10 degrees results in significantly greater stress on the heart, lungs and legs.

Gently rolling terrain is preferable to one long march up a hill and one down, since the forces on the legs will be different going up hill than coming down. **Alternating uphill with downhill avoids overstressing the legs.** Begin this program at the same mileage as you ended the first phase (same for you and same for the horse, if they were not). You will also have become more sensitive to how hard the horse is working and can use these tools to design a work load and gauge his progress as your conditioning program moves on.

Rider check-out

Many of us tend to put on a few pounds when we're not riding. Extra weight will affect your balance and make both you and the horse work harder, so it is a good idea to make some effort at weight reduction. Something simple like giving up your favorite sweet or junk-food snack or switching to spring water instead of soda will often significantly reduce total caloric intake and reward you with a gradual-but-noticeable weight loss.

And it is just as important to get your muscles strengthened and tendons and ligaments loosened up as your horse's.

Exercises for the rider

Riding is a great way to burn calories and tone the body. Unfortunately, the specific areas that require the most strength and flexibility are those where many people have the most problems: back, hips, pelvis, thighs and hamstrings. Jumping right back in the saddle will quickly let you know how much work these areas need. It is safer — and more comfortable — to begin a strengthening and flexibility program before you start riding again. These simple exercises target key areas and will help you get in shape.

As with any exercise, don't overdo it at first. Sore muscles will set your conditioning program back.

Calves: Both strength and flexibility in the calf muscles and the Achilles tendon (running down from the calf muscles across the back of the leg and heel) are essential to a secure seat and correct position of the lower leg. Walking works this area effectively, but you can get a head start by including more trips up and down stairs, using a stair-climber device or simply standing on the edge of a step, balanced on the balls of your feet, and allowing your heels to drop down as far as they will go, then standing up on "tippy toes." Ten repetitions, two to three times a day, work great.

Back, hips and thighs: A secure seat and effective use of the rider's weight requires that the back, hips and thighs have flexibility. They must be able to work as a unit or independently. We prefer exercises that gently work and stretch all of these areas at the same time.

1. Pelvic tilts. Lie on your back, small of back pressed against the floor and feet flat on the floor with knees bent, lower leg perpendicular to floor. Tighten your thighs, contract your buttocks and lift and tilt the pelvis upward and forward. You will feel the small of your back press into the floor as your buttocks and hips lift up and forward. Do 10 repetitions, two to three times a day.

2. Back curls. Lying flat on the floor, bring your knees to your chest and hug them tightly. Begin to gently rock backward and forward, as if your curved spine were the bottom of a rocking horse. This exercise allows you to quickly identify any "knots" (areas of spasm) in the muscles surrounding your spine.

When you come across a spot that is sore or more firm along your spine, repeat rocking with a more limited range of forward and backward motion until the knot begins to smooth out. (This really works!) Do 10 complete forward-and-back rocks, two to three times a day.

A variation on this for the more flexible folks is to bring your knees to your chest then straighten your legs and attempt to touch the floor behind your shoulders with your toes. Sounds exotic, but this is a great stretch for the lower back and spinal muscles.

3. Frog-legged stretch. This is a terrific stretching and strengthening exercise for the hips, back, pelvis and thighs. Lying flat on the floor, bring the soles of your feet together, reach forward and grasp your toes, slowly lie back down as you bring your legs to a position perpendicular to the floor, keeping the soles of your feet together and allowing the legs to assume a frog-legged position. This tilts the pelvis forward, opens up the angle of the hips, stretches the inner thigh and is a wonderful stretch for the lower-back area and spinal muscles.

Hold the position for 10 to 15 seconds, breathing slowly and avoiding any muscular contraction in your back, hips or thighs. You will feel your lower back and inner thighs stretch and the small of your back press tightly against the floor. **PH**

15

Conditioning The Older Horse

Basic rules of safe conditioning should be followed with a horse of any age, but senior citizens returning to the work force have some special needs and concerns.

Before you seriously consider bringing an older horse back into work after a lay-off, he should be carefully examined for physical problems. Checking old lamenesses/injuries is the most obvious place to start. Make sure these are not bothering him when you begin your exercise program. Some type of game plan may be required along the way to help minimize the chance of reinjury and to keep the horse comfortable.

Lungs

The horse's soundness of "wind" (ability to breathe well and deeply) could also affect a conditioning program. There are no breathing problems particularly associated with age *per se*; that is, lungs don't necessarily get worse with age. **But a lifetime of exposure to respiratory viruses and irritating plant/grain dusts and molds — not to mention environmental pollution if that is a problem in your area — can combine to make the older horse's breathing capacity not quite what it used to be.**

If the horse has a history of breathing problems, have your veterinarian listen to his lungs before and after a little bit of work prior to starting a conditioning program. Even if the problem is not serious enough to keep you from working the horse, it could interfere with your ability to accurately determine how hard you are working him (see monitoring vital signs). Your vet can also give you a list of signs to indicate if the lungs are being too irritated or that the horse might temporarily need medication.

General management and diet

Preplanning in the dietary and general management departments can save headaches and setbacks farther down the road. Unless the horse is already too fat, you may need to change his diet to allow for the extra calories needed to work. Often this means the addition of grain or an increase in grain. **The basic diet should include 1.5% of the horse's weight as hay for the early parts of the conditioning process** (15 pounds or about one-third bale of grass hay for a 1,000-pound horse). Many horses will hold their weight quite well on this until work levels exceed 30 to 45 minutes per day of trotting on the flat or more strenuous work.

When weight begins to drop, or when the work level exceeds a half hour or so at moderate speeds, you will need to either increase the hay or add grain. Using grain is generally a more reliable way to both control calories and make sure the horse is getting what he needs (a lot of hay gets wasted and stomped on, making it hard to tell how much was eaten). **Begin adding one to two pounds, two to three times a day.** For horses getting a very high-quality hay, particularly if it includes alfalfa, a 10% protein grain will work just fine. If hay quality is not so great, go with a 12% protein feed.

Try to choose a feed that is readily available in your area so that you can keep his diet constant. Use a feed formulated for horses at your horse's level of work. The longer the list of guaranteed vitamin and mineral levels on the tag, the more heavily fortified the grain will be. Levels of protein, fat and fiber are required by law; other levels are usually voluntarily guaranteed by the manufacturer. If they are on the label, the state feed regulatory labs will routinely check to ensure the feed measures up to its promises.

Wait five to seven days after any change in your horse's diet to determine if it will be adequate to maintain his weight. If he needs more, increase at a rate of one to two pounds per day, maximum, and again wait a reasonable time to determine if that increase is enough.

You will have to step up your grooming routine to keep the horse's skin healthy and free from sores or rubs. If the horse has an extremely long coat, it might be wise to clip his lower legs (so that small cuts don't get overlooked) as well as the saddle/girth area.

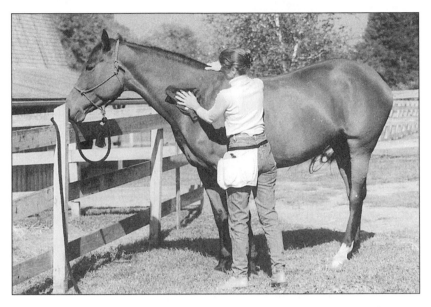

You might begin your conditioning program with a thorough grooming. Not only does it help promote circulation to the horse's skin, but vigorous massage may help condition the muscles (and help you get in shape) as well.

This is a real time saver in keeping these important areas as clean as they need to be.

Hooves need special attention. Have the horse trimmed and shod in a way that is appropriate to the type of riding you want to do. If your hoof care program has become a little lax, get into the routine of daily cleanings. Add hoof dressing, if necessary.

Think ahead about first aid for the working horse. **It is a good idea to keep a container of poultice around for bruised feet or minor leg problems.** You should also have a few clean leg wraps in waiting and know how to use them.

Foam shipping wraps or stall bandages can double as cold leg wraps for sprains, if you soak them in ice water. Another good way to keep cold therapy ready-to-go is to fill a few various sized ziplock bags with shaved ice and keep them in your freezer. These mold easily to anywhere on the leg (as does a bag of frozen peas) and can be held in place with an Ace or regular bandage. Ask your veterinarian about the advisability of adding a syringe of phenylbutazone paste to the supply list.

Monitoring vital signs

Learning to check your horse's pulse and respiration is the best way to monitor how hard he is working and to avoid over-stressing him.

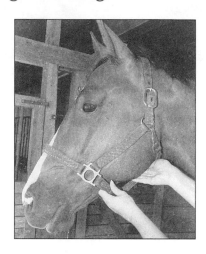

The pulse is usually taken from the horse's facial artery, which runs along the lower edge of his jaw. Feel for the artery by pressing your fingers lightly but firmly along the edge of the bone at the back of the jaw and running forward until you feel them bump over a round structure slightly less than the diameter of a pencil. You will be able to roll the artery around somewhat. To take the pulse, place your fingertips lightly over the artery (not hard enough to push it away) and wait until you feel a pulse. Count the beats for 30 seconds and double the result.

The horse's resting pulse will be somewhere from the high 20s to the 40s. *A horse is considered to be doing "light" work when his pulse remains in the 60 to 150 beats per minute range over a 15-minute period. This is a broad range, however, and probably too much to safely expect of any older horse. Excitement, confusion or pain can falsely elevate the pulse when you first start back to work. If your horse's pulse seems higher than it should be and does not respond to regular work by gradually dropping as he becomes more conditioned, look for a source of pain.*

A reasonable pattern of heart-rate response for an older horse would be:
First and second week — pulse 60 to 80 maximum
Third and fourth week — pulse 80 to 100 maximum
Fifth and sixth week — pulse 100 to 120 maximum.

A pulse of 150 after 15 to 20 minutes of work is considered moderate work for horses in general but could actually be hard work for an older horse, and a rate of 120 is probably safer to consider as moderate for this age group.

Your horse's respiratory rate (breaths per minute) is also a good indicator of how much he is being stressed. The respiratory rate is subject to the same "false" elevations as his pulse. That is, excitement or pain will cause it to go up. You do not need to actually count the breaths per minute to get a rough idea of how hard the horse is working. When the horse is working lightly you will be able to see the nostrils flare slightly with each breath and may begin to hear his breathing.

As work progresses to moderate, the nostrils will obviously flare a bit with each breath, and movement of the chest wall will be more obvious when the horse comes to a stop. Breathing is clearly audible. The horse whose nostrils flare wide open, who makes loud breathing noises and whose chest heaves has been worked heavily — too heavily for an older horse early in a conditioning program, and possibly too heavily for an older horse, period.

If you notice hard breathing even with light work, especially if the horse's pulse rate remains in the expected range for light work, the horse may have a breathing problem, and you should get a veterinary examination before going any further.

Special considerations for the older horse

Older horses do not become fit as quickly as younger animals. Their muscles, joints, ligaments and tendons are not as resilient. The older horse has also usually lost some muscle mass, and his joint cartilage is not as thick and healthy as in a younger horse. **It is especially difficult to bring an older horse back to a fit condition after a long lay-off.** In many cases, the horse simply will not be able to do as much or as hard work as he could before. This does not mean he cannot be worked, only that your expectations might have to be dropped compared to his younger days and that you need to be especially careful when beginning work again.

Most older horses also come with one or more problem areas in their legs. Pay close attention to any signs of lameness/discomfort when you work the horse, and check the areas by feeling for heat or swelling every day. Checks should be made before you begin riding, as soon as you are done, after the horse has been cleaned and cooled out, and the last thing every day. **Signs of heat, swelling and pain may not become obvious until a few hours after the horse stopped working, or even until the next day.** It is usually possible to "work through" flare-ups of old problems, provided you catch them early enough and treat them appropriately. Icing and wrapping should be done at the first sign of trouble. Get advice from your veterinarian on how to proceed from there.

If your horse has an old joint or tendon problem that makes him move stiffly all the time but is not really "flaring up," heat is the therapy of choice. Use such things as massage and light liniments, bandaging and Neoprene sweat wraps. These will all increase circulation to the area and help to keep it "loose" and moving as freely as possible. A low-level exercise conditioning program will also work wonders in restoring free movement, as long as you are careful not to overdo it.

Planning a conditioning program

Every horse will be different in terms of the amount of exercise he can tolerate after a period of inactivity. It is important to estimate what he can tolerate easily before you plan an exercise routine.

The best way to do this is to work the horse from the ground in a round pen or similar small enclosure where you can control him and his rate of movement. **Work the horse at a relaxed trot for 10 minutes, then immediately take his pulse, and note general indicators of stress** (how hard he is breathing, degree of sweating). If his pulse is 60 or below, he can tolerate this easily. If it is up to 80 or so, this is plenty of work to start with. Do this for two or three days, or until the horse has obviously become a little bored with the idea. You will then have a good indication of how to begin.

Next, perform the same level of work with a rider on board. You should have someone on the ground take your horse's pulse or be able to hop off quickly and do it yourself. Carrying a rider will be more work overall, so expect the horse's pulse to be somewhat higher than before.

When first conditioning your horse, work him without a rider. You can use this slow, light work to improve his responsiveness to ground-handling cues, which will be an enormous help once you start riding.

Your first week of work should probably be done in a paddock or arena where it is easy to monitor the horse's response. Ten to 20 minutes of walking and trotting with a rider is a good place to start. This is an excellent time to practice "giving to the bit" and asking the horse to make specific movements, like moving his shoulders or hips over. **That way, your control improves before you ask your horse to work at faster speeds.**

Use a duration of exercise that keeps the horse's pulse in the desired range as we discussed. Most horses will quickly adjust to exercise at this level. As soon as the pulse begins to drop, you can increase the time spent riding. By the end of the second week, the average horse will be up to 30 minutes of walking and trotting (start with walking a few minutes, and walk breaks are a good idea, too, every 10 minutes or so).

Spending the first two weeks this way will get you off to a good start and with a pretty good idea of how much work your horse can safely do. At this point, you can trail ride — either for the same times and at the same pace or for longer times at a slower pace. **Increasing**

the duration of work is generally safer than adding speed. Use your next week or two of conditioning to safely bring the horse up to working 45 minutes to an hour and doing it comfortably within the safe heart rate/pulse zones.

After a month of this type of careful, slow conditioning, your horse should be ready to take on faster work for short periods (five to 10 minutes to start) and longer periods of more moderate work (over an hour). **Make all changes gradually and check the pulse after each period of fast work to make sure you are not over-stressing the horse.** This is the time to gradually introduce the more specialized and difficult types of work, if that is your goal (sharp turns, lateral work, sliding stops, jumping). Again, 10 to 15 minutes of the "tough stuff" is enough to start. If you follow this plan carefully and don't let yourself be fooled into overdoing it by a horse that seems eager to do more, by the six-week mark you will be well on your way to safely bringing the older horse back into his best possible condition. **PH**

Section II

Perfectly Practical
Advice About
Riding

16

Riding On The Road

Preparing your horse to handle the hazards of roadside riding can help keep you safe in unexpected situations. We'll walk you through the basic cues and maneuvers you and your horse need to know.

O ur first choice for a riding area is a beautiful green field, or perhaps a shady trail, open plain or even an arena with great footing. But for many people who can't ride right off the farm and onto the trail, it's either ride along the road to get to the trail or arena, or don't ride at all. Unless your horse is trained well enough that you can control him, "not at all" is your safest option. But since that defeats the purpose of having a riding horse, let's look at how to train your horse to be safest when riding on the road.

Riding along the roadside is potentially far more dangerous than riding within an enclosed area. In addition to traffic whizzing by, you often have limited space for turning your horse around or getting him under control if he gets upset. Often, the footing is poor and the ground uneven. Culvert pipes, trash and broken bottles lurk in the weeds, ready to snag an unsuspecting horse. Add the challenge from dogs and bicycles, and you'd better be ready to help your horse handle the hazards. Before I even think about riding a horse on the road, I make sure that I've taught him a number of basic control exercises. No matter how good the rider, there are some horses who shouldn't be ridden along the road.

That's because it takes more than just ordinary training to keep your horse safe on the roadside — it takes having taught your horse emotional control. We've all had the experience of having to deal with a horse who performed perfectly at home but then got upset away from home, or who was fine on the trail until his buddy was ridden away. **It's when the horse is stressed that we really find out how well conditioned he is to our cues. We have to train three parts of the horse — his mental recognition of our cues, his physical responsiveness to the cues and his emotional control.**

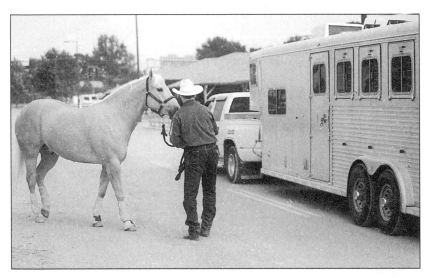

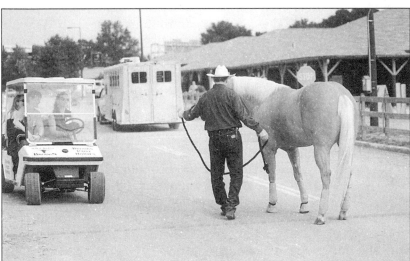

John took advantage of this opportunity at a horse show to accustom Trouble to being around vehicles. He'll practice leading lessons before riding Trouble in the same area.

Prerequisites

Because riding on the road is so potentially dangerous, be honest with yourself about the amount of control you really have. We'll just mention the various cues or exercises that you should be able to do with your horse before you consider heading onto the highway.

It should almost go without saying that you should be able to stop and turn your horse easily, from most any gait and from either side. But since most people tend to ride more often one direction than the another, and they work on turning one way rather working on each side, they often assume they can control or turn their horse both ways. You have to specifically train your horse, however, to respond to each rein separately.

The most important cue to have down pat is the "turn your hips" cue, or what I refer to as "connecting the rein to the hips." When we can move the horse's hips, we can control his direction. So we pick up one rein, thinking about the horse moving his hips to the opposite side, then we release that rein when he moves his hips. With practice, the horse moves his hips as soon as we ask.

We use the rein to talk with the horse's hips, rather than using our seat or leg, because the rein is easier for the horse to understand and easier for us to use, and it's actually a stronger cue. **The more out of control a horse becomes, the more important it is to use just one rein and to control the horse's hips.**

You want to be sure that your horse knows the "speed up" cue; when you kick him, he should know to move forward. Many people just lean forward or release the reins to tell their horse to go forward. That works fine when the horse already wants to go. Then those cues tell the horse, "OK, that's fine with me."

But what happens when he balks or doesn't want to move? The "speed up" cue tells the horse, "I'm going to keep bumping your sides with my legs from now until forever or until you move your feet, whichever comes first." With practice, the horse learns that you will stick with the cue, and that you'll stop bumping as soon as he moves, so you develop a cue he takes seriously.

Along with the "speed up" cue is the "slow down" or "stop" cue. Nearly everyone can stop their horse if he's walking. Most people can stop a horse who's trotting, but few really have control when he's loping or galloping. That's usually because they've never really practiced stopping from the gallop, or if they did, they stopped when it was convenient or natural for the horse. The faster a horse moves his feet, the more excited he usually becomes, and that's where the emotional control is necessary. The horse may know the cue to stop, but if his excitement overrides his conditioned response to the cue, you don't have any brakes. **In order to teach our horses to be calm, we have to get them excited, then calm, excited, calm — we can't just keep them calm. We have to condition the calm-down muscles, as it were, for them to work when we need them.**

IF THE HORSE BECOMES AFRAID, TURN HIS FACE TOWARD THE TRAFFIC, NEVER AWAY. HE COULD EASILY BACK INTO WHAT HE DOESN'T SEE.

One way we can do that is by teaching our horse to drop his head on cue ("calm down" cue). When a horse is excited, his head is up. When he drops his head, his excitement or fear level drops momentarily also. After training the "calm down" cue, if something frightens your horse — and you can just about bet, if you ride on the road for very long, something will — you'll have a cue that forcefully tells him to relax. When you are faced with a traffic scare, no amount of sweet talking or relaxing your seat will tell your horse to relax. His focus will be on the scary object or sound, so you need a no-nonsense cue to tell him to calm down.

To train the "calm down" cue, we take slack out of the rein, focusing on the tip of the horse's ear. We keep pressure on the rein until the ear begins to drop, then we release the rein, telling the horse he did what we wanted him to do. Through practice, we can actually reverse the horse's natural tendency to raise his head when he feels pressure on the rein.

The other aspect of training that few people think about before heading out on the trail is leading manners. **We often take our horse's leading manners for granted — we allow him to bully us a bit or to push into our space as long as he's not wildly out of control.** But if he barely responds to leading cues when he's calm at home, he'll likely ignore them when he's away from home and excited. At the very moment when you most need control, you are least likely to have it.

Introducing him to traffic

Once you've worked through the prerequisites at home, the next step is to ride him in a pasture that borders a quiet road. If you don't have a situation like that on your farm, try to trailer your horse to a place that does. Going to a new place will raise the excitement level, and you'll get a more accurate idea of how good your control really is before you venture out onto the busy road.

Begin by riding about 60 feet inside the fence, so you are a distance from the road. Ride facing oncoming traffic. This will be a key factor in all your road riding. **You always want the horse to face a scary object; you never want the object to come up behind him.**

As a car approaches, be sure your horse is facing and looking toward the car. As the car begins to pass you, turn your horse's front end so his nose continues to face the car and he can watch the car go away. When the car has gone a distance away, pet the horse, and turn him around so he's ready when the next car approaches. If the horse begins to get upset, don't fight with him — either ask him to drop his head or ask him to move his hips over, so that he can continue looking toward the car.

Once you feel he's going to be OK with the traffic that passes in that situation, turn your attention to riding and working on exercises as if you were at home.

Choose one exercise to work on. I normally think first of the "connect the hips to the rein" lesson, because that's what will give me the best control in nearly any situation. So I'll walk, then ask the horse to move his hips over, then release the rein and ask him to walk again. I'll ask again, this time with the other rein. When he's doing super at the walk, then I'll work on trotting and stopping.

As the horse moves his hips, you'll find that he almost does a turn on the forehand, which means that at least one front foot stops momentarily so he can pivot on it. If when you ask him to move his hips, you think about stopping and you release the rein as he begins to move his hips, he'll get the idea of a one-rein stop. So now you can practice trot, stop, trot, move the hips and so forth, and really gain great control. That way, if the horse gets scared and begins to trot off, you've already practiced the stop-from-excited-trot cue.

It's important for you to be the same rider when away from home that you are at home. Even though the horse gets excited, you have to keep your focus. Don't change your cues, and don't get angry with him if he seems not to remember lessons that you've worked on. That's normal. Fear and excitement often make thinking difficult.

Also, only practice the same lessons that the horse does really well at home. This is not the time to teach him something new.

Once you feel the horse is responding as well in this new situation as he does at home, move closer to the fence (and the road),

John rode toward this vehicle, and as it passed, he kept Trouble's nose facing it. In the photos above, John is turning Trouble to where he can be in position to see the next car come along, and he praises Trouble for a job well done.

continuing the same exercises. The purpose of the exercises is not just to improve his responsiveness to your cues; most importantly, you're working on getting the horse in the habit of keeping his mind on your requests. That way, he'll learn to focus on you instead of the traffic.

If you can't find a situation inside a pasture fence, then you might try working from the ground and practicing leading lessons, particularly the directional control (WESN) lesson (in which you tell the horse to go west, then east, then south, then north, using lead line cues) and practice the same "control the hips" lesson with the horse wearing a snaffle bridle with a lead rope attached to the bit ring. (**You have more control with a snaffle than a halter.**) To introduce your horse to traffic, lead him to the end of your driveway and do the same lesson as we described earlier — face the oncoming traffic and then continue facing it as the car goes by, or go to a local horse show where you can train as folks arrive with their trailers.

On to the roadside

For your first real roadside ride, choose a road with little traffic and few other distractions. The shoulder should be relatively wide and flat so you don't feel crowded or hurried. When I first ride my horse on the road, I don't necessarily ride with someone else (though you may want to have a friend in a car nearby). That's because when my horse gets excited, he's far more likely to focus on the other horse than on my signals, and my safety depends on his responsiveness.

Continue the same training as you did in the pasture, keeping your horse occupied with your requests, but facing traffic, turning and following the cars as they go away. **Don't let the horse just stand and look at traffic; in fact, the more out of control the horse becomes, the one thing you do not want to do is tell him to stand still.** Keep him busy with simple tasks — giving to the bit, moving his hips over, walking forward two steps then moving his shoulders over as he keeps walking, then moving them back, then moving his hips, and so forth — not high-intensity requests, but in such quick succession that the horse doesn't have a moment to think about anything but what you're asking of him.

If the horse becomes afraid, turn his face toward the traffic, never away. He could easily back into what he doesn't see. **When the horse makes an out-of-control move, your first objective is to get him under control so that you can then make a logical decision to stay on him or to get off.** Your safety is the most important consideration.

Now an hour into this lesson, John keeps Trouble facing traffic, but he works on moving his hips over. This is a more difficult setting because there is a fence on the horse's left, so there is nowhere for Trouble to move to if he gets scared.

At any point, if you don't feel safe being on your horse, step down. If that horse is going to step in front of a car, as awful as the thought is, it's better that he do it without you on board.

Here are some suggestions about how to handle the "what ifs" you will inevitably run into:

■ **If he wants to spin — work with his hips, not his front end.** The horse's front end is already "light," but the hind end powers the move. Keep asking those hips to move over. Keep him facing the traffic.

■ **If he's going too fast — if you can't control his speed by moving his hips over and asking him to stop periodically, then get off.** This is often the case when you're headed home and he gets into a fast walk. Rather than fight with him or ask him to change directions and so forth, you'd be better to lead him and let him calm down. I don't want my horse overheated and exhausted, and I don't want to ride him in an out-of-control situation.

If I think the situation is safe and I want to work with him to slow him down, then I'll first ask him to speed up in the gait that he's already offering me. For instance, I'll ask him to walk a little faster than he really wants to. Then I'll offer him the chance to slow down.

If he doesn't slow down, I'll ask him to speed up at the walk, and so forth. After a few times, if you offer him the chance to slow down for three or four steps, he'll take it. You can build on that.

Or I'll work on changes of direction. I may not be able to do a 90-degree turn, but I may be able to do a smaller change of direction (not a curve, but a change). So every time the horse speeds up, I'll ask him for a change of direction. I change left and right, ideally not two rights in a row.

The one thing I don't do is try to "hold him back." That's like driving with your foot on the brake. The brakes will overheat and become useless. You have to give a horse a release somewhere. To do that, change directions or move his hips over, and give him a split-second release from the rein, even if you have to do it again a moment later. But don't release unless the horse has done something. Just pulling and letting go at random isn't like pumping the brakes — it won't work.

■ **If the horse locks up and won't go past something — recognize that he's stopped where he feels relatively safe.** Don't press him to go closer to the scary object until he's dealt with his fear; otherwise, you're likely to push him out of control. So if he freezes 40 feet from a mailbox, don't kick him. Instead, pet him and tell him he's OK and that you won't let that horse-eating mailbox get him. Let him know he's safe with you.

When we bump (kick) our horse, that's our cue for him to move his legs. But the horse who balks isn't ready to move, so there's no sense giving him the cue.

When I think my horse is relaxed enough to move his feet, then I'll bump him gently with both of my legs — smooth, rhythmic bumping. If he backs up, he's moved his feet and I'll quit kicking. Most likely he won't move, so it's good that I didn't decide to kick him hard, or I'd be kicking hard until forever or until he moved (according to my "speed up" cue contract, when I first taught it to him).

If I've started bumping him with my legs and he hasn't moved, I'll keep bumping, but I'll also pick up one rein (toward the street) and tell the front foot to move to that side. The moment the horse picks up that front foot, I'll quit bumping, and I'll give him a mini-release of the rein.

If he starts to turn around like he's headed for home, then I'll pick up the rein (away from home) and make him face the mailbox again. I won't turn him in a circle to face the mailbox, but I will make him go back the way he came. That way the mailbox won't be behind him (and perhaps chasing him, in his mind). No matter how far away from the mailbox our dance takes us, I'll use the rein to turn his front end or hind end to keep him looking toward the mailbox, making sure to give little releases when he does each step right.

Depending on the situation, I may or may not go by that mailbox on this ride. If I have to go past the mailbox (for instance, to get to the trailer), then I'll work on a series of exercises (either from the ground or the horse's back, whichever is safer), starting at least 40 feet from the mailbox. When the horse performs great at 40 feet away, then I'll move to 38 feet then back to 40, then 36 and back to 38, and so forth, making sure that I have excellent control. My objective is to get the horse past the mailbox safely — it is not to get the horse to put his nose on the mailbox — so I'll work on exercises that get us past the mailbox. Eventually, we'll work up to where we can ride right by the mailbox without him getting concerned about it.

Professionally speaking

We asked Darlene Geiser, mounted police trainer, to share some of what she's learned in years of police work, particularly advice on riding along the highway or amid traffic.

Perfect Horse: *What considerations do you keep in mind when you ride on the road?*

Darlene: *I stay as visible as I can. I wear reflective gear even in daylight; I wear contrasting colors — white shirt and dark pants, for instance; and I ride facing traffic.*

PH: *Isn't riding toward oncoming traffic against the rules?*

Geiser: *When I ride facing traffic, people always holler at me that I'm going the wrong way. They just don't know it's the right way for me and my horse. That's because most people aren't aware that a person riding a horse is technically considered a pedestrian in most states. This means that, just as when you're afoot, you should ride facing traffic. Pedestrians have the right of way, although many drivers don't acknowledge this.*

A carriage, on the other hand, is considered a vehicle, so horse-drawn vehicles should travel in the same direction the traffic does.

PH: In your experience, what is the main cause of traffic accidents involving horses?

Geiser: Usually accidents result either from lack of training or lack of common sense. When horses get scared, they do what comes naturally. For instance, a group of riders riding along the road should go single-file. Then, when one horse crosses the road, all should cross. If only one horse crosses the road, the other horses will try to follow, and they either end up fighting with their riders or they wind up out in the road.

The other problem occurs when horses aren't accustomed to traffic before they go on the road.

PH: How can you get a horse used to traffic without going on the road?

Darlene: Along with your usual training, you can get him comfortable with car horns, lights, engines, car doors and so forth,

Retired from the Jacksonville, Florida, police department, Darlene Geiser now travels throughout the country training mounted police units. Her horse, Bold, has won numerous awards, including National Police Horse of 1995. Bold became a Breyer horse model in 1997.

right in the arena, where he's in a safe place. You can develop a whole training program, bringing the vehicles around the arena. Park cars together and (when your horse is sufficiently trained) walk him between them. Some horses don't like to go through narrow spaces. That fear will endanger you on the road, for instance, if the horse has to pass between bushes and the road or a parked vehicle.

Then, too, you can drive a noisy, rattling trailer around the arena. That always gets a horse's attention. See if you can keep your horse's attention despite the distraction.

When police horses first go out on the street, even after all their training, one of the things that bothers them is when a UPS driver opens the side door of his truck and suddenly appears there. (So re-enacting a similar situation with a van in your arena is a good idea.) There's no such thing as a "bombproof" horse, but the more training you can do at home, the safer you'll likely be if you have to ride on the road. ▣

17

Marking The Trail

Whether you manage a small boarding stable with access to a few miles of trails in suburbia or you ride on 1,000 wilderness acres, trail markers make the ride more enjoyable and perhaps more safe.

The scene is familiar. You've just finished watering and feeding all of the horses in your boarding barn but one. You are ready to close the barn and head home, but that last horse is nowhere to be seen. Finally, a horse near the end of the barn whinnies in the direction of the state game lands. You hear an answering whinny in the distance. Squinting against the last rays of the setting sun, you can see that a horse and rider are making their way along the pond trail.

"I took the wrong turn," says the rider as he unsaddles his mount. "I ended up over near the high school. Guess I just don't know the trails yet." You promise to set aside time to ride with your new boarder to show him more of the local trails, wondering how you'll fit it in with all your other chores.

Plastic/paper dinner plates are easy to write on and staple to trees or onto stakes. They make great trail markers both for riders and to advise vehicle traffic on private roads.

Endurance riders depend on trail markers to identify the competition route.

Proposing solutions

You've drawn good maps for your boarders, but no one remembers to carry them. You've tried to institute a buddy policy, but people's schedules don't always mesh, and some folks like to ride alone. You've set up a sign-in-and-out board, but that doesn't help the rider who may be lost.

How about marking the trails? After all, you've had no problems following the flowing, brightly colored ribbons marking the trail at the Spring Thaw Endurance Ride for the last couple of years.

Questions enter your mind as you head to the house. Would the local landowners appreciate you decorating the trails that they so kindly let you and your boarders ride? How long would ribbon markings last? What sort of permanent markers would be acceptable but affordable?

To help sort out this dilemma, we explored several ideas for trail markers. As you read, you may decide to use one of these systems or think of more possibilities, perhaps even combining systems.

How the pros mark trails

Biltmore Saddle and Bridle Club (BSBC) of Asheville, N.C., manages several competitive and endurance rides throughout the year, as well as hunter pace and combined training events. BSBC has developed a multiple trail system utilizing colored plastic arrows stapled to trees, fence posts and free-standing stakes, when necessary. Each trail has a different color.

Even when there is no competition, there can be as many as 100 riders on the Biltmore trails, as more and more trail members spend weekends camping. With an active lesson program, staff members could not keep up with direction requests, so the permanently marked trail system, using red, white, blue, yellow and green arrows, provides trails varying from 8.5 to 26 miles in length.

What trail markers can do

Trail markers can be subtle, like the signs at national parks, or bright, so riders can't miss them. Both have their place, but it's important to use the trail-marking system that works best for your situation, then explain to the riders what it means. Unless a lost rider knows what a brightly-colored streamer means, he's just as lost as without the marker.

Generally, trail markings should be eye level from the rider's viewpoint, which is usually also high enough not to attract the attention of vandals. Trail-marking convention for endurance rides puts the marker on the right whenever possible. That works great when there's a plan to go from Point A to Point B, but what if you use the same trail out and back?

We suggest if there is more than one trail, you name the trails or at least areas of the trail. That way a rider can tell you he's "going around the lake" or "taking the blue trail" and you'll know which direction he went. If the blue trail has all blue markers, it's simple.

It also makes giving directions easy. If someone is injured on the trail and you tell the medical crew the injured rider is "up the hill on the blue trail just past where the pink trail crosses," there's a good chance help can get there quickly. Or you could meet a hiker at a certain time and place for a picnic lunch.

Another approach is to use different colored ribbons to indicate going toward or away from home. "Red on the right" may mean that you are headed home. Conversely, if you see the white ribbon on the right, you know you are headed away from the barn.

Trail markers can also indicate hazardous spots, maybe where the ground is always soft or where a big hole is not usually visible because of fallen leaves.

If you use markers that can be written on, like plastic plates, you can warn riders of hazards, such as a big dog that likes to jump out at the horses. If you change plates often and carry a waterproof felt marker, you can even leave a note for riders coming later in the day.

In all trail marking, consistency is paramount. Markers should be about the same distance apart, whether every 50 yards or every quarter mile. However, when riders know what to look for, only the turns or trail crossings need be marked. A good idea is to place a "confidence marker" just after the turn to let them know they are on the right path.

Ribbons

A ribbon marker can be of any length, but about 18 inches is recommended for the best visibility. Good reasons for using ribbons (surveyor's tape) include availability, low cost (about $1.35 for a 250-foot roll), ease of installation and high visibility, provided you use colors that don't blend with the scenery.

Trail-ride managers we contacted agreed that fluorescent pink is one of the most visible colors year-round, with white the next-best choice. Ribbons are hung at consistent intervals. Turns are usually marked with a "flurry" of three sets of ribbons, hung on the side of the trail in the direction of the turn.

Ribbons are best for trails used for a specific purpose or for a short time, like a weekend trail ride, though we have seen markers that have been in place for years. Ribbons tied tightly to tree trunks can eventually kill the tree. If you are planning to remove the markers after a ride, attach them to spring-type clothespins to speed up marking and un-marking the trail.

Marker ribbons are an invitation for vandals, both human and animal — for some unknown reason, cattle and deer are intrigued by them — so there is a natural attrition rate in ribbon markers. And, if fluorescent pink ribbons don't meet with your neighbors' idea of a natural environment, you will need to consider other options.

Signs

Signs can be attractive, which is an advantage. Permanent signs can be made of wood, plastic, tin-can lids or even horseshoes. They can be installed as stand-alone fixtures or fastened to trees. Prior to making permanent signs, try the marking system and location of signs with temporary markers.

A low-cost option is tin or aluminum can lids, painted with a color that can be easily seen but not blatant and nailed to trees. Of course, permission to nail or staple anything to trees must be secured from landowners first or trail privileges may be lost.

Plastic dinner plates are good for making long-lasting signs, and they can easily be cut into shapes, like arrows. They are easy to tack up with a staple gun and can be used to provide information when written on with permanent ink. A plate marked with a black "X" is universally understood to mean, "Don't use this trail."

Permanent signs can be written on or engraved — or attractive, discreet shapes can tell the story.

Used horseshoes are a low-cost and long-lasting solution, but they are a bit difficult to carry along the trail on marking day. Another factor to consider is that horseshoes require fairly long nails.

Rocks

The first trail marking in prehistoric times, other than slashes cut into trees, may have been rocks. Rocks are usually plentiful in most areas, a distinct advantage. Single rocks can be painted to provide a fairly unobtrusive and permanent marking system. Rocks can be arranged in an arrow shape to point the way, although in modern times this might be an inviting target for trail sabotage.

One competition trail manager set up the trails so that the painted rocks could be turned over after the event, since that trail was not used throughout the year.

Glowsticks

Glowsticks, available in camping-supply stores, are great idea for an evening trail ride. These non-toxic, non-flammable fluorescent green lights cost under three dollar each, last about 12 hours and have a highly visible soft glow. Glowsticks are about eight inches long, about 5/8" in diameter (fatter than a pencil) and have a loop through which you can thread plastic tape. To make them glow, you shake them, then snap them once to mix the chemicals inside. When tied to trees they are easy to see at night, lighting the trail as well as marking the route. The down side is that they require someone to set them out prior to the ride and someone to pick them up at the end.

A Glowstick can be tied to a tree trunk with surveyor's tape.

Safety first

Obviously, the reason we're talking about marking the trails is safety, not just convenience. But, whether or not trails are marked, riders should familiarize themselves with the local terrain. Is there a creek or river? What direction does it flow in relation to the barn?

Short-cut trails home should also be learned and marked. The issue of whether the rider or the horse is learning the trails is not

particularly important, but, in fact, the horse usually learns the way home more quickly than his human companion. **PH**

*Our thanks to contributing writer
Barbara Madill*

A black X is the universal signal indicating that a trail is closed. This might be a helpful code for days when the trail is exceptionally muddy and you don't want it torn up by horses passing through.

18

Low-Impact Trail Riding

*Whether exploring the wilderness deep
in the back country or taking a leisurely
afternoon ride on community trails,
we all must be good stewards of the land.*

Those of us who enjoy trail riding must become more aware of our lasting impact on public lands. Two organizations in particular — Leave No Trace, Inc., and Back Country Horsemen of America — have developed minimal-impact strategies for enjoying the great outdoors with our equine companions and for helping to preserve our trail-riding privileges.

Careful preparation is key to an outing that is friendly to the environment. First, contact the appropriate agency — the area rangers' station or park management — for local regulations and recommendations. Ask about trail access, limits on group size, grazing allowances, campfire usage, bear guidelines, rules about dogs and so forth.

Obtain maps of the area and plan your route, charting roadheads, river crossings, campsites and alternative sites. Also, consider weather conditions to avoid riding when the environment is especially vulnerable. During rainy season, for instance, traveling on muddy trails and soft ground can create erosion problems.

Preparing your horses

Your horse should be healthy, physically fit and trained to be responsive to your cues. An out-of-control "Nervous Nelly" can quickly rip up the terrain, whether pawing when tied or spooking at things that go "bump" even in daylight hours.

These experienced trail horses, eating out of feed bags or on a tarp, are tied on a highline as an elk passes by in the background. It takes training and preparation for this to happen.

Of course, the sight of unfamiliar wildlife (elk, moose, bear) and trail companions (llamas, loose dogs, dirt bikes and fully loaded hikers with packs swaying above their heads) can unravel the most reliable of mounts. A refresher course of "spook-in-place" training could help avoid major wrecks.

Before you set out, familiarize your horse with as many new camp sights and situations as you can think of, including tents, saddle bags and rain slickers. Be sure he'll cross streams, bogs and puddles quietly and remain calm in confining spaces, such as on narrow paths or when coming upon downed trees. Also, practice mounting and dismounting from both sides — you may find yourself in a position where you can't turn around, such as on a ledge or hillside. If you intend to take pack animals along, be sure both you and your horse are comfortable with managing a pack string.

Since pawing and trampling is particularly damaging to soils and plant roots, teach your horse to stand tied quietly for long periods. However you intend to confine him — whether with hobbles, picket line or portable electric fence — try it at home first.

If hobbling, be sure your horse has been trained to wear hobbles, that you have done all the spook-in-place work, and that he's thoroughly bomb-proof when it comes to ropes around his legs, things dragging off him and so forth.

To prevent introducing non-native plant species to the environment, feed your horse and pack animals processed weed-seed-free feed and hay for several days beforehand (gradually shift to the new feed to avoid colic) and bring it with you to feed while camping. Some areas may be heavily overgrazed or have little forage; in other especially fragile areas or where local wildlife need the forage for themselves, grazing horses may not be permitted. In states that require weed-seed-free feed, local feed stores usually stock certified hay and feed; otherwise, any heat-processed feed or hay pellets (not hay cubes) will typically contain few viable seeds.

Finally, check your gear for proper fit. A horse with a sore back, mouth or cinch area may become unruly.

Gearing up

As you pack, take only what you know you'll need. Plan your meals and food proportions to minimize waste, and repackage food in reusable containers to reduce trash.

The popularity of backpacking has fueled the development of extraordinarily lightweight camping gear, from cookstoves to clothing, rain gear to sleeping bags. By keeping your gear weight and mass to a minimum, you decrease the number of horses and pack animals needed, which means less trampling of trails and campsites, plus less feed to pack in and less manure left behind.

On the trail

While charting a new course may sound exciting and romantic, it can be unnecessarily destructive to the natural ecosystem. Stay on established trails. Cutting switchbacks tramples plants and loosens soil, which can lead to eroded gullies and muddied streams and lakes.

To keep from widening the trail, ride single file, and don't allow your horse to skirt around muddy patches, puddles and low obstacles. Clear away deadfall across the path to prevent the creation of secondary detour paths. If you do need to leave the trail temporarily — for a rest stop, for instance, or to let another group go by — look for trample-resistant ground, such as a dry meadow or a sandy spot.

Key concepts for
low-impact trail riding

To escape the routine of arena-riding, horseowners frequently saddle up and head for the hills, the forests or the high country. Thoughtless trail riders often leave behind substantial damage, including girdled trees, overgrazed meadows, eroded shorelines and fly-attracting manure piles. As a result, angry hikers, bikers and backpackers have successfully lobbied many public parks and wilderness areas to ban horseback use.

■ *Minimize trampling of plants, soils and shorelines. Ride single file and stay on the trail (no shortcuts!). Choose hard ground for campsites. Cross creeks at established fords.*

■ *Confine your horses with highlines or portable electric fences. Don't tie horses directly to trees.*

■ *Don't introduce non-native plants. Only pack in grain and hay that is free of weed seeds (also use it as feed for several days prior to your trip to prevent spreading undigested weed seeds via manure).*

■ *If you pack it in, then pack it out. Leave nothing behind but footprints (and keep those to a minimum).*

Setting up camp

Since plants and soils are more fragile above the timberline, try to set up camp below the timberline whenever possible. **When selecting a campsite, a good rule of thumb is to use a well-worn site and thus avoid enlarging the area of disturbance.** In remote areas, however, a lightly used site may return to a natural condition if left alone, so in that case, it's best to start afresh elsewhere.

When selecting a new site, look for an area of hard, dry ground. Put the camp's kitchen area, which receives the most traffic and impact, in the most resilient spot. Also, some land-management agencies require that campsites be located at least 100 feet from water's edge; others require 200 feet (about 70 adult steps) or more. The bigger the buffer, the better.

While in camp, don't build "improvements" such as wooden shelters, lean-tos, tables, pole corrals or hitchrails where none already exist.

Especially on well-used trails with established campsites, firewood is frequently scarce. A lightweight gas campstove can eliminate the need for firewood; just be sure to pack out your empty fuel containers.

Where campfires are permitted, gather only downed, dead firewood. Do not cut off or break down branches, even on dead trees; pick up loose branches already on the ground. Only use wood no bigger than a human wrist — small branches will burn down to a fine ash.

Abide by standard fire-safety guidelines (never leave your fire unattended, do without a fire in windy or dry conditions, etc.). When breaking camp, be sure that fires are out cold. Then, sprinkle the dead ashes over a wide area, away from the camp site.

Call ahead to inquire about disposing of human waste. While urine poses little harm, some land managers may require you to pack out all human feces, which can contaminate the ground and nearby water sources. In that case, pack a good supply of plastic bags. Otherwise, do your business in a "cat hole" at least 200 feet away from the campsite, trails and water sources.

When washing dishes (or yourself), keep all soaps away from water sources. Use as little soap as absolutely necessary (even biodegradable soap breaks down slowly), and carry wash water at least 200 feet away from lakes and streams to scatter it. Remove any food scraps first, however, and pack them out to keep from attracting wildlife to the camp.

To set an example and encourage others to use the same site, leave all campsites clean and attractive. Never leave litter (including cigarette butts, candy wrappers, twist ties, etc.) or food scraps behind. Scatter manure piles to hasten decomposition. Fill in all pawed holes.

Take-alongs

In addition to common camping supplies (i.e., matches, first-aid kits, maps, compass, whistle, camping gear, Coggins papers, etc.), these tools will help minimize your impact on the trail:

■ *Highlines with tree-saver straps, a portable electric fence, hobbles*

■ *An ax or small bow saw to clear deadfall off the path*

■ *A small trowel/shovel for digging cat holes and for breaking up manure*

■ *Nose bags and collapsible water buckets*

■ *A lightweight strainer to remove food particles from dishwashing water*

■ *A pair of tennis shoes to soften the impact of foot travel in camp (however, never ride with tennis shoes in stirrups)*

■ *Plenty of insect repellent (hoof stomping, pawing and rolling can damage the terrain)*

Confining your horses

Horses should ideally spend as little time as possible in camp, just long enough to unload and load up. Keeping them at a distance not only disperses impact, but also cuts down on dust and flies in camp, as well as manure underfoot.

Avoid tying your horse directly to trees. In addition to chewed-up bark, pawing and trampling can damage underground root systems. If you must tie up temporarily (while preparing more suitable confinement, for instance), choose a tree with at least an eight-inch diameter trunk (a tree this size can usually recover from some disturbance).

Whenever you tie up to a tree, protect the trunk from rope rubs with tree-saver straps made from wide nylon belting (wide dog collars do nicely, too). You can also wrap the trunk first with a cushioning fabric, such as burlap grain sacks.

The best option for tying horses for periods of an hour or more is a high picket line, strung about six or seven feet high between two trees. A highline is less likely to break than a chest-high picket, while giving the horses less of a sense of entrapment, allowing them to walk and turn around under the rope.

To site your highline, choose a flat, hard area where the least ground cover will be disturbed. Avoid soft, marshy spots. Look instead for dry areas that catch breezes to reduce biting insects and lessen pawing and stomping.

Highlines must be stretched taut: Experienced trail riders recommend using half-inch hemp or multi-filament poly-plus rope (nylon is often too stretchy). Tie your horses' lead ropes to the highline with the halter snap about two feet off the ground, which will let your horse lie down without getting tangled (a swivel snap will keep the lead from twisting as your horse moves around). Knots should be hard and fast to prevent the leads from sliding up and down the highline and keeping the horses from chewing and trampling around the tree trunks.

Know your horses' natural pecking order and tie them accordingly, keeping buddies next to each other. Spacing can vary, depending on the temperament of the horses, but 10 or 15 feet is usually adequate.

When planning to camp in one spot for a couple of days or more, a portable electric fence, one that operates on batteries or solar power, can make a good temporary corral. However, it's safest not to leave horses confined in an electric fence at night in the wilderness. Put them on a highline before dark.

With any confinement, the smaller the area, the worse the impact. Often, the best method of restraint for experienced horses is hobbling, which gives the horses the freedom to spread out and disperse impact.

Realize that a horse can travel quite a distance wearing hobbles, so you'll want to secure a perimeter. Always keep at least one horse tied near camp. That way if the hobbled horses leave, they have someone to come home to (and you have a way to go search for them). Last, but not least, secure anything in the camp or surrounding area that a loose/hobbled horse could get injured on. That would

When possible, ride single file and stick to established trails to minimize impact on the terrain. You can imagine the damage if these horses spread out and traipsed across this meadow when the ground was soft.

include camp gear, any kind of fuel or poisons — things you would not necessarily think of as trouble may be risky.

To reduce the risk of overgrazing, restrict grazing time to about three hours a day on good grass. Allow your horses to graze down no more than 50 percent of available forage. To minimize foraging, pack in weed-seedless processed feed and hay pellets. Nosebags will help reduce waste and pawing. If you choose to feed on the ground, however, put the feed on top of a tarp to minimize feed loss and ground-cover damage.

When leading your horse to water (a nearby stream or lake), look for an established ford or low bank with firm footing. Try to minimize trampling around the shore. When possible, use a water bucket to keep your horse from muddying the water and trampling sensitive vegetation.

Leave no trace

Follow the philosophy "If you pack it in, then pack it out." Never leave garbage, cans, aluminum foil (which won't burn), grease, paper or food scraps. If you can, try to pack out trash left behind by other, less conscientious campers.

Finally, take as many photos as you like, but leave wildflowers, natural objects (interesting rocks, antlers or petrified wood) and historical artifacts, like arrowheads, alone. In many areas, removing anything is illegal. Every choice you make today may affect whether you'll be allowed to return tomorrow. **PH**

Our thanks to contributing writer Liz Nutter
Photos courtesy Back Country Horsemen of America 888-893-5161

19

Don't Ride That Buck

John fills us in on the all-important topic of bucking
— how to prevent a buck, how to see it coming,
and what to do to make sure
your horse isn't a rodeo prospect.

I do not ride horses that buck. If someone I'm visiting hands me a horse and says, "He's a nice horse, but he bucks a little," I don't get on that horse. It doesn't matter who else is going on the trail ride or what wonderful scenic places the ride may take us by. I never figure that I can ride better than the horse can buck, and I don't assume that because he only bucks a little with someone else, it will be OK for me to ride him. And I certainly don't think just because I've ridden a horse that bucked and lived through it, that it's wise to do it again.

A buck isn't determined by whether the person falls off. It's determined by the actions of the horse. When he humps his back and has an "attitude," I consider that a buck, whether his feet really left the ground much or not. **I'm not getting on that horse until I feel reasonably sure that he's not going to buck.**

Wearing the horse down before he's ridden won't assure me of that. Some folks lunge horses to get rid of "excess" energy. I don't want to lose my horse's energy; I want all the horse's energy available for the ride, for learning something new or for improving performance. If a horse really wants to buck, a little time on the lunge line won't keep him from bucking. But developing control might.

As soon as I get on any horse, I formulate a plan as to what I'll do if he should spook or become upset. When I begin riding and asking him to give to the bit, I determine which side he gives to the best. That will be the rein I use to control him. So, for instance, I'll

This horse isn't bucking to be mean — he's scared of the saddle and the stirrups.

tell myself, "If he spooks or starts to buck, I'm going to pick up the left rein and move the horse's hip to the right." That way I don't lose critical moments thinking about what to do when I could be getting the horse under control.

But the best thing I can do is to prevent a buck in the first place. **If I think there's a possibility that a horse may buck when I'm on him, I'll work with him from the ground.** I put a snaffle bridle and reins on him because I'll want him responsive to the rein once I'm riding. (To the horse, the rein is the same whether I'm on his back or on the ground.) So working from the ground allows me to teach rein cues without endangering myself by getting on him.

Why horses buck

Most of the time, when horses buck, it's because they're scared. I assume the first year a horse is ridden that he may get scared and buck. That doesn't contradict what I said earlier about not riding bucking horses. If I think the horse is likely to buck, even a little bit, then I work him from the ground to get him responding to cues and to build his confidence. But once I've done everything I can from the ground, I stay aware that something may still frighten him and that his natural reaction may well be to buck.

What prompts a buck?

Often, things you don't think about set a horse off. For instance, let's say that every day you take a soda out to the ring and put the can on the fence while you ride. One day you take iced tea instead of soda, and when you pick up the glass, the ice cubes rattle. Your horse spooks, and in a moment he's off and running. Or a dog jumps out of the bushes when you're on the trail, and instead of your horse having a "heart attack," he bucks. Or maybe you stop riding to unwrap a sandwich, and he reacts like a rattlesnake is on his back, instead of just plastic wrap and bologna. People tend to think of these horse wrecks as freak accidents, but they are normal parts of life — a horse doesn't know that, however, until he's more experienced.

And just because a horse is 15 years old doesn't mean he's experienced enough to not buck when startled. If he's only ridden once in a while or if his training was inconsistent, his coping skills may be no better than those of a three-year-old barely broke horse.

Sometimes a horse who's been ridden for years will get scared, too. Often what happens is that a horse may handle a big scare well, but afterward, he gets especially reactive to movement or noise, spooking over things that never bothered him previously. That horse isn't being bad or "stupid" — he's genuinely afraid.

I went through this with Zip after taking photos with a helicopter. He did just great at the time of the photo shoot and didn't appear unduly worried. But the next symposium, he "bugged out" at the same American flag we'd flown at every symposium he'd ever been to. It took a while to get him over that.

We should take precautions to help our horses get over their fear, and until then we must make sure we don't put them or ourselves in situations where we could get hurt. You can't just tell a scared horse to "cowboy up"; you have to backtrack in his training until he's over his fear.

Out of control

While being scared or startled is the most common reason that horses buck, the other reason is that the rider has gradually lost control, usually without realizing it. Instead of the rider determining what the performance standard will be, he lets the horse do whatever he wants, as long as it isn't a big problem. Then "suddenly" he finds the horse out of control.

John has just asked Seattle to move his hips to the right. He's given him a mini-release and is preparing to ask for a second step.

For instance, let's say that one day the horse drags his feet about leaving the barn. The rider has to kick him and steer a bit, but the rider is busy chatting with friends and doesn't take the horse's actions too seriously. The next day, the same thing happens. The third day, the horse is a bit more pushy, but the rider doesn't think much of it and lets the horse stop because they are waiting for another horse. The fourth day, the rider has to kick him harder, but he thinks it's because the horse's buddy is not going today, and on it goes. "Suddenly" on the fifth day, the horse refuses to leave the barn area. The rider can't understand why and thinks that the horse has never done anything like this before, when in reality day-by-day he'd been excusing the horse's behavior instead of directing it.

In this scenario, the horse became increasingly more adamant about getting his own way, but the rider was oblivious to the horse's resistance because he was able to coax the horse into doing what he wanted without a crisis. **In fact, many riders think that a little resistance like that is normal, and they don't recognize it as a problem in the making.**

Then, instead of blaming their own lack of control, the rider usually labels the problem as barn- or buddy-sour, or they blame some other distraction (i.e., he was just vaccinated yesterday and he didn't feel well). **In reality, the problem is that the rider failed to give the horse specific cues and to enforce early on that the horse obey them.**

Or let's say that the horse didn't "act up" in the driveway but continued on out onto the trail. At some point along the trail, the horse decides he's not going to respond to a cue — for instance, to cross a road — and he exhibits the same behavior he's been doing at home for two months. But this time, because of the situation or excitement, the rider's demands are more intense, or they both get scared because the footing isn't good — and the wreck is on.

The same kind of situation happens when novice riders buy an experienced horse to learn from. The new owner forgets or doesn't really know that he's supposed to tell the horse what to do. Left on his own, more or less, the horse begins making his own decisions.

So, for instance, if the horse is faced with deciding whether to stay on the rail in the arena or taking a shortcut across the ring, what do you think makes most sense to the horse? Obviously, cutting the ring. So the great rail horse is now on the rail going down the long sides, but adamantly cutting 10 feet off each end of the arena, and the skill-less rider is powerless to fix it. Ten feet becomes 15, and the rider decides he needs the help of a trainer. The riding instructor tells the rider to "get after him" and to make him go to the end of the arena. And suddenly, the horse bucks.

Or folks sell their "problem" horse and then buy a trained trail horse. But instead of keeping the horse thinking about what the rider wants, the rider lets the horse do what he wants. Before too long, the new horse is exhibiting the same behavior the old one did. **For instance, instead of controlling the horse's speed heading back to the barn, the rider assumes that since it's only a fast walk, that's OK.** When instead of walking, the horse begins to trot, then trot fast, the owner decides that might not be OK, so he tries to slow the horse down. The horse begins to jig because he wants to get back to the barn, just like he's always done. The rider gets scared and decides that he's going to get that horse under control right now, so he turns the horse away from home and — you guessed it — the horse bucks.

Back to the classroom

In each of these cases, and hundreds more like them, **the key to preventing a buck is recognizing that the rider must be in control.** The rule is: **Ride where you can, not where you can't.** Ride the horse in an environment and attitude where you're pretty sure the horse won't buck and where you can direct his behavior. If he bucks on the trail, don't take him on the trail until you've retrained him to all the basic cues and until you're sure you have better-than-great control of him in a non-threatening situation. Go back to a training program where you're not worried about the trail or other people and their horses.

First, set a performance standard — a medium-speed walk, let's say, in a straight line away from the barn. Don't assume that any horse should walk a straight line away from the barn at a medium speed unless you've taught him to do that.

Recognize that your goal isn't the starting point. You may have to work on walking, stopping, walking, stopping, walking fast, walking slow, walking fast, stopping, walking fast, and so forth, in lots of other places before you ask him to do it away from the barn. Then you may have to work on direction control, so that you can steer left and right well enough to keep your horse on a straight line. **When the horse responds well to your cues in both calm and exciting settings, then try to walk him away from the barn.**

Exercises to practice

■ **"Give to the bit."** *Teach the horse that when you pick up on the rein, you want a part of his body to move. The term "give to the bit" doesn't refer to a head position, but to a physical movement accompanied by an attitude that says, "I'm eager to do what you tell me."*

■ **Move the hips with the rein.** *This is a variation of the "give to the bit" lessons. We want to be able to pick up one rein, hold tension on it and have the horse move his hips over to the side. If you learn to do only one thing with the reins, this should be it.*

■ **Speed control.** *Going at the right speed doesn't mean keeping the horse from going too fast — it's a matter of teaching the horse to go fast and to go slow, whichever and whenever you tell him to. If your horse suddenly ends up going 10 mph because something scared him, you'd better have practiced going from 10 mph to 3 mph in a safe setting. If you've only ridden at 3 mph, and your brakes are only practiced at 3 mph, you won't be able to stop your 10-mph horse.*

■ **"Calm down" cue.** *This is a demand cue that tells the horse to drop his head when you pull hard on one rein. When a horse is excited, his head is up and he's harder*

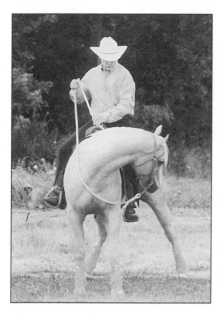

This horse would have a hard time bucking because his hip can't power him up or forward and step left at the same time.

to control. Like all cues, it must be specifically taught so that the horse knows the difference between one rein that says "move your hips," and the same rein that says "drop your head."

■ ***Turning.*** *Contrary to what most people think, circling does not necessarily slow a horse down. If you want a horse to stop going north, you have to turn him away from north, for instance, and head due west or south. That means practicing turns that are 90-degree or more. You can practice circles all day long and still not be able to turn your horse when you need to.*

What is your cue?

You really have to ask yourself what cue do you wish the horse responded to better. For instance, if your horse doesn't slow down or steer easily, you'll have to work on responsiveness to rein cues. If he balked or didn't go forward, then you have to work on "speed up" leg cues. If his head was too high or he attempted to rear or fight with the bridle, teach him the "calm down" cue, so you can tell him to drop his head and relax on cue. (**Horses do not buck just because their head is down, nor will keeping a horse's head up prevent him from bucking.**)

Most control problems boil down to horses who won't go forward or who won't stop, turn or drop their head. If you have a horse who backs up, what is your cue to tell him to go forward? Backing isn't the problem; his not responding to your "go forward" cue is.

He bucked suddenly

Unless genuinely startled or stung by a bee, few horses buck suddenly. Most have been sending signals that they're getting frustrated or scared, but the rider didn't pick up on the warnings. And unless the horse is really scared, if he bucks suddenly, it's because we missed something in his ground training.

Maybe we know, for instance, that he's headshy, but we think we just have to live with it or that he'll "outgrow" it. Then, when we bend forward to go under some trees, he bucks. We think it's because we may have touched him with our legs as we bent down (which may be true, but if he bucked because of that, we didn't do a good enough job sacking him out or in our basic riding training). Instead, the horse probably bucked because he thought we were about to touch his ears.

Learn to recognize the signs that your horse is beginning to get out of control, and then regain control before you have a fight. **If your horse speeds up but you haven't told him to do so, he's taking matters into his own hands. If you haven't told him to move his hips to the left but you're going sort-of sideways down the trail, he's telling you he has something other than trail riding on his mind.** Don't ignore your horse and intervene only when he's doing the wrong thing. Tell him what you want before his mind wanders. By asking him for performance as you go down the trail, you can make sure he's thinking about your priorities, not his own.

If you think your horse may be getting worried or contemplating high-tailing it home, tell him to move his feet in the direction you want them to move before he moves them on his own. Replace his thought with your thinking and, in the process, improve his responsiveness to some cue. Ask him to move his hips to the left or right, for instance, or tell him to drop his head or change gaits. **You may have to ask him to move his hips over 20 or 30 times, but as you ask him to do something and then reward him for doing it, he'll begin thinking more along your lines, without a fight.**

Imagine that you're in a car with a kid who's been irritating you with *Star Wars* special-effects noises from the back seat. Knowing he likes math, you ask him, "What's 6 times 7?" When he says 42, you tell him, "Great. So how much is 8 times 4? How about 12 times 6? And 4 times 42? I'll bet you don't know what 24 times 12 is," and so forth. When that happens at rapid-fire speed, both you and the child have fun; he's engaged; his math performance improves, and the special effects disappear — all without scolding.

If Seattle shook his head, threatening to buck, John would have him make a 180-degree turn, then immediately tell him to move off into a canter. If he threatened to buck again, John would again have him turn, then move right off.

If he bucks

The better the horse's training, the less likely that he'll ever buck. But since we can't assume that the horse will never get scared and then buck, we have to know how to deal with it.

When a horse bucks, his hindquarters power the move. So our "defense" is to disengage his hindquarters as quickly as possible. The easiest way to do that is to get the horse to move his hips over. If I think a buck is coming, I'm going to reach down and grab one rein with both hands (remember, I've already determined which rein that will be). I'll quickly pull that rein hard (but I won't jerk it) until the horse moves his hips over. Then I'll immediately release the rein. He'll no longer be going forward. Then I'll determine the next step. If I think it's safe to get off, I may do that.

If I think the horse is going to move again, I'll do the same thing to the other side. If I first pulled on the right rein, telling his hips to go left, I may release the rein, then immediately slide both hands over to the left rein and pull that, telling the horse's hips to go right. If I think I may lose control in that moment when the horse's head is lined up in front of his body, then I'll repeat the request on the same side.

Whichever side I'm working on, though, I always release the rein, even if only momentarily, when the horse moves his hips over. If I don't, he will fight harder. He won't know a release is available, and he'll feel he gets pulled on no matter what he does. So that split-second release is key.

If I'm on a horse who doesn't respond well to one side or the other, then I'll stay with the rein that he does respond to. **My objective is to limit the horse's forward movement and his ability to buck.** It isn't to teach him a lesson or show him who's boss — it's just to keep us safe. I'll do my training at another time, perhaps even a few minutes later, but only when I know he'll be able to concentrate on what I want and that we can both stay safe. If I think the horse will buck again, I'll walk him home (even hand-walk him, if necessary) and practice there, until I'm as sure as I can be that he's not going to buck.

He bucks when he lopes

The horse who bucks as he goes into the canter or once he's cantering is a slightly different situation than the other bucks we've talked about. The causes are the same — he's either afraid, or he wants his own way and the owner has conditioned him that he can get it. The difference is that the warning sign is usually specific — the horse shakes his head — and, of course, everything happens much faster than at the walk.

What usually happens is that **the horse shakes his head (like he's saying "NO") just a step or two before he bucks**. So, by watching for that sign, you can prevent the buck. If you are riding along a fence, pick up the rein closest to the fence (or use the side he gives to best, if you're not in an arena) and pull on that rein until you get a change of direction. Then make the horse move off quickly. If he does it again, change directions again. **Every time he shakes his head like he's about to buck, make a 180-degree turn, kick him and ride him off at a fast trot or canter.**

Practice lots of speed-control exercises at the trot — for instance, fast trot for 20 steps, then slower trot for 20 steps, then faster trot for 15 steps, and so forth. When you can get the horse to do a really nice stretched-out trot, then encourage him to go just a little faster, then a little faster. He'll start wishing that his feet didn't have to move so fast, and he'll slip from an extended trot into a slower canter. This time, his attitude in the canter will be different because he'll want to slow his legs down, so bucking won't be on his mind. ■PH■

20

Foul-Weather Riding Tips

*Riding in the rain and mud need not be problematic
if you plan ahead and observe some
foul-weather and problem-terrain tips.*

Finally, a few minutes to ride. As you tack up, you scan the sky. Rain clouds are gathering, but you know there are no thunderstorms in the forecast. With advance planning and certain techniques, riding in the rain and mud can be almost as much fun as riding in the sunshine.

Rain to horses is as natural as sunshine — at least in their free-roaming state. **In a driving rain, they'll want to turn their tails into the wind, but otherwise, rain probably isn't going to be a big deal.**

If it begins to rain as you're riding and you want to don your coat as you go, be sure to keep hold of the reins. The noise and movement of a flapping coat can unnerve and spook even a calm horse. It's not

Dressed for rain: Long coat that covers the saddle and lets rain run off the shoulders; boots and gloves, plus a plastic cover for the hat.

177

hard to hold the reins while you unfold the coat, and you can switch hands on the reins while pulling on the sleeves. Be sure that your horse has been thoroughly sacked out and that you've done lots of putting the coat on and taking it off at home in the arena before you try it on the trail.

This is extra important because as the rain comes up it may be windy, and you may be hurrying to avoid getting too wet. If the horse is already excited and you have any doubts, dismount to don your coat. If you're riding with friends, be aware that excitement in one horse will excite the others. (This is where your "calm down" cue comes in handy — tell your horse to lower his head even when the other horses are on alert.)

A roll, anyone?

After the rain, when the horses are steamy and damp, be alert for signs that your horse may want to roll, even with you on board. This is particularly important if you've brought beginners or children along, because they may not be alert to the signs of an impending roll.

Horses will naturally look for a dry place under the loose top layer of soil to roll in (we've all seen this tendency after bathing a horse). You'll usually get a warning in the form of pawing (sometimes, it's only one paw and down-she-goes!). If you sense that your horse is thinking about rolling, keep him busy. You might tell him to step sideways, trot or just move him on down the trail.

Lightning

When on a ride, designate a storm spotter to pay attention to the possibility of a thunderstorm. Lightning often comes along the leading edge of a storm, frequently prior to the rain. If you can, get to the safety of a barn or shelter. Once inside the structure, go to the middle and do not touch the walls or fixtures.

If caught outside, avoid exposed open areas, tall trees, wire fences and any place where the electrical current might be attracted to an object and travel through you on its way to the ground. Avoid situations where you and your horse are the tallest objects around. Get to a low-lying area, like a little valley or even a ditch. Dismount and move away from

*your horse (a rope halter without metal parts and a long
lead is helpful here). Other riders and horses should do the
same, moving away from each other.*

*If you get caught out, and a single tall tree is the only
object around you, avoid being under the tree or out in
the open where you are as vulnerable as that tree. Look
for a grove of trees with one tall tree, and take shelter in
the grove but far from the tallest tree. Avoid running for
home, as lightning has been shown to be attracted to
moving objects.*

Cold and wet concerns

Beware of 35- to 45-degree temperatures when it's raining; this is
not only uncomfortable, but can be dangerous. Hypothermia is the
condition where your core body temperature drops because body
heat is being lost more quickly than it is being generated. Sports,
such as riding, where you're relatively inactive but have gotten
sweaty (for example in an impervious rain coat), can make you a
victim. Children, with their small body mass, are particularly sus-
ceptible. A cool wind across your wet clothes can rob you of whatever body heat you've accumulated. The most obvious sign of
impending hypothermia is uncontrollable shivering. After that, you
may notice that your coordination decreases (you can't untie your
coat, or it's difficult to shorten your reins).

Before you get too cold, get off and walk. If you're going for a
longer ride away from home, a first-aid kit with some energy food
is an excellent safeguard. Foods high in carbohydrates will help
warm you long enough to ride back home.

**Horses can also suffer from hypothermia. Wet and cold condi-
tions, combined, are particularly risky because horses' hair does
not provide good insulation when it's wet and flattened against
their bodies.** A period at the trot (on good footing) should help warm
the shivering horse.

Mud and boggy spots

We've all been frustrated at one time or another by a horse who
refuses to step into a puddle in the driveway. We know the footing
is solid, but he may not. With training, your horse will obey you,

but we can also take advantage of the horse's ability to determine what is risky and what is not.

When faced with the possibility of a boggy or muddy crossing, stick to known safe routes. When in unfamiliar country, look for cattle or deer tracks (the more recent, the better).

Avoid areas that are both rocky and muddy, particularly if the rocks are angular, because a slipping foot may come into contact with a sharp rock.

Get to know your area. You'll find that there are regional and local variations in the consistency of the mud — from quicksand-like traps to soft areas with firm terrain underneath. Sometimes the firm terrain will give good purchase; in other cases, it will be treacherously slippery (for instance, during a thaw when there's slush on top of frozen ground). In some areas, you'll learn to recognize the different vegetation that grows in passable and impassable spots.

There are times when it's fine for your horse to jump a little ditch or muddy spot, but other times the banks aren't solid enough or the landing involves a sharp turn or a low-limbed tree. And, of course, he should only be jumping under your direction, not out of your control.

When crossing a stream or boggy spot, follow the footprints of other animals and allow your horse time to find his own footing.

Use rainy day practice to get your horse to walk rather than jump. As he approaches and enters the obstacle, restrict his forward movement to walking steps. While training, ask him to cross narrow streams or muddy stretches at an angle lengthwise along the stream to make it easy for him to walk through and harder to jump across.

When riding in a group, give the leader plenty of space and look for alternative crossings if his or her choice wasn't particularly successful. Where the leaders stop while waiting for the remaining riders will influence how easily you'll be able to keep your horse's attention on his work. (If you choose a different crossing upstream from the group, it will be helpful if the leaders move upstream on their side.) **By contrast, their leaving in a downstream direction may make it harder for you to get your horse to concentrate on his footing if he thinks he's being left behind.**

During rain, or when rain is in the forecast, avoid steep canyon-like areas and dry riverbeds that might flash flood if enough rain falls upstream. Flash floods are just that: Sudden. They can occur even in relatively arid areas like the Southwest.

Watch those shoes and tendons

We've all heard that mud sucks off a horse's shoes; usually this is only when they're loose to begin with. **A shoe lost in the mud happens when the footing is deep enough that it slows the exit of a front foot, and the hind foot reaches forward and steps on the shoe heel.** You can minimize this by letting the horse pick his way through deep mud at a slow pace.

If you'll be faced with mud, snow or ice on a routine basis, talk with your farrier about the advantages of your horse being barefoot, or of wearing shoes with greater-than-average traction. If you're serious about needing traction flexibility, ask about screw-in caulks (the caulks can be removed or changed for others appropriate to the surface — mud, grass, etc.). **Understand that any shoe that increases traction also increases the suddenness at which the horse's foot stops as it lands — this is a stress to his joints that you may choose to avoid.**

Mud is a real danger in terms of pulled ligaments and tendons. When his foot slips out from under your horse, the motion can stress a ligament or tendon. You can prevent most of this by adjusting your pace to the footing — walk when necessary, and avoid galloping and jumping. Prevention also comes in the form of prior planning — avoid changing pace, gait or direction in a slippery or deep area.

Also, avoid such transitions any time the surface changes — from dirt to hard pack, sand to grass, and so forth.

Plan ahead so you can slow to a walk before your transition has to occur on the new and potentially more dangerous footing. **Remember, too, that transitions in questionable footing will take longer for your horse to execute, just as it takes your truck longer to stop on wet pavement or on a muddy road.** Watch far out ahead of your horse; if you don't know the area well enough to predict when the trail will turn muddy, take it easy the whole way.

Slicker wisdom

You'll need a place for your rain coat on the saddle: Add straps if your saddle doesn't have saddle strings. Tie your coat on with enough bulk on the outside of the strings so the strings won't slip off the coat. This may necessitate rerolling your slicker until you get a long enough roll. Don't be afraid to crank down on the strings: a firmly tied coat will be less likely to slip out of the strings. If you use the saddle strings a lot, or if they are old, expect some wear. Rather than risk an accident when your slicker comes loose and flaps, or comes off, replace any worn or aging strings. They can be replaced relatively easily on many Western saddles; you may even be able to do it yourself.

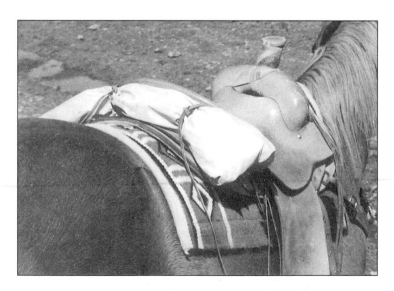

Mud and hills

Horses are actually quite sure-footed in mud, and sliding hooves do not have to be a problem. Your horse does not want to fall any more than you do. Going down a slippery slope, if you feel his feet sliding, sit quietly in balance and support him as he is accustomed (some may prefer light rein contact; others will prefer to be left alone). Regardless, don't get busy with your reins (he couldn't stop if he wanted) or with your balance (don't make him adjust to your changing balance as he is trying to balance himself).

Stay at a walk, even if he wants to hurry. **Keep his nose pointed down the hill; the worst thing you could do to his balance while your horse is making his way down a slippery slope is to turn him sideways across the hill.** He can safely slide — even with all four feet if necessary — straight down, but when he is positioned sideways to the hill, and his feet start sliding sideways, his balance is in jeopardy.

Going up hill, close your hip angle (move your belt buckle closer to your pommel or saddle horn) to put your weight more forward over your horse's changing center of gravity. Give him enough rein to stretch his neck down for balance, and let him dig his toes into the mud. **Walking is less likely to pull tendons than faster gaits.**

After the ride

As after any ride, be sure to pick out your horse's feet, checking for rocks and making sure that his shoes are secure. During your grooming, be alert for any cuts or scrapes that might have come from rocks in the mud or a hind foot overreaching and catching a front heel. Run your hands down his legs to check for heat and swelling that might signal a pulled tendon.

Be sure to hose off the mud and dry his lower legs thoroughly to avoid the chapped skin that is a precursor to the bacterial and fungal infection called grease heel.

If he worked hard enough to get hot and sweaty, and it's a cool day, be sure to cool him down gradually like you would any athlete. Avoid standing him in drafty areas. Start with a cooler draped over his whole body, and fold sections back from his head and forward from his tail as those parts of his body dry and return to normal temperature. This process, accompanied by hand-walking him, rubbing him with dry towels, and even, after strenuous exertion, giving him a few swallows of lukewarm water at intervals, helps his muscles return to their pre-ride status with less stiffening and cramping. Ensuring that his body temperature has returned to normal before you leave him will prevent his re-heating and sweating (particularly under a blanket, if he wears one) and the resulting chill that comes from standing with wet hair on a cool and/or windy day. Enjoy this time with your horse, and be sure to watch for rainbows after the storm.

Equipment and clothing

Tack considerations:
Leather saddles and bridles need periodic conditioning and oiling anyway, but if you're going to subject them to rain, it's all the more important. If you keep your leather well-conditioned, you won't have to oil your tack before a ride in the rain, or worry about it being damaged as it dries. Leather with a good oil content (not oily-feeling, nor dry, but pliable) won't absorb as much water as neglected leather, and it will dry more quickly.

Soaking up lots of rain and then drying out again is more of a stress to leather than just getting damp is. Getting leather damp won't hurt it; you do this on purpose when you clean it. If your tack is suitably oiled, you probably won't have to do anything special to it after the ride. Let it dry naturally — don't hang it near a heater because the heat will leave it stiffer and more brittle. If your tack was a little light on oil before the ride, or if it got soaked, you can use a light coating of conditioner before it dries completely, and then you may need to reapply an oil product after it dries. Let the feel of the leather be your guide.

Leather reins get slippery when wet, so try reins with rubber overlays, or a braided or flat web nylon for the rainy season. If you use a mecate, try horsehair or a rougher grade of nylon; braided cotton gets heavy and stays wet long after the storm. Maybe you have a "rainy day bridle," or you can just swap out the reins.

Rain wear: *Choose gloves that give you a good grip on the reins, like those with rubber on the fingers and palm. It's nice if they keep you warm even when they get wet — try wool or one of the synthetic wicking fabrics.*

Leather chaps or chinks (the short version of chaps) will let the rain run off your thighs. They are good with a coat that covers your saddle (otherwise you'll have a pool of rainwater at your seat!). Some riders prefer rain pants instead of chaps or chinks. Rain pants will help keep your seat and lower legs dry, and add a layer of insulation against the cold. Some are slippery, particularly if they weren't designed for riding, and others won't breathe in the summer sun — making you wet on the inside — so shop carefully.

If you ride in the rain in your leather riding boots, you'll have drying out, cleaning up and oiling to do when you get home. Slip-on rubber overboots are available in different heights. Don't sacrifice safety for comfort, though — oversized stirrups are available if your muck boots are wider than your regular boots.

Consider getting an inexpensive plastic hat cover. And a stampede string — cords from your Western hat that meet under your chin — will prevent your hat flying off in the wind. While your horse should already be accustomed to strange objects flying at him, and should have learned to tolerate your hat being waved and bumped all over his body, a stampede string should keep the hat on so you don't have to get off and chase it.

The challenge in choosing rain wear is that it must keep you dry without making you sweat. If it's cold out, sweating is not a problem, but in warmer rain, plastic rain wear can make you just as wet as the rain alone would.

Fabrics, such as GoreTex, that allow sweat to escape while keeping rain out are useful. If you choose an oil-skin coat, be sure it's been waterproofed lately.

If you take a non-riding friend along on your quiet horse, be sure to tell him or her to bring appropriate rain gear. While many outdoor enthusiasts use ponchos in other outdoor sports, ponchos are not appropriate for riding because they catch in the wind and create a "sail" effect. Ponchos are also difficult to mount in — you can't see your stirrup — and can catch on the saddle when you dismount. If you're stuck with a poncho as your only option, you can make it work by tying a baling twine belt at the waist. PH

Our thanks to contributing writer Sue Stuska, Ed.D.

21

Rider Down

*Knowing what to do — and what not to do —
after a rider takes a tumble can mean the difference
between recovery, crippling injury or worse.*

I t can happen in a heartbeat. A horse stumbles, spooks or bucks, and suddenly a rider hits the ground, hard. What you do in the next few moments to help your fallen friend can have lifelong effects. Would you know how to handle the situation?

We talked with Doris Bixby-Hammett, M.D., of the American Medical Equestrian Association, who walked us through the basic steps in a rider-down scenario:

■ Immediately stop all nearby horse activity so the fallen rider doesn't get trampled or forced to move. If the rider's horse is running off, let him go or let someone else catch him — your first priority is to help the fallen rider. Make sure your own horse is out of the way, too.

■ Determine whether the rider needs medical attention. If so, or if you aren't sure, call 911 or your local emergency number immediately.

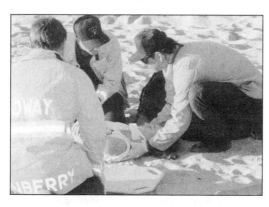

Paramedics are trained and have the right equipment to move the fallen rider without causing further injury.

Stay calm, reassure the rider and shield her from sun as necessary. Avoid excessive activity.

■ Unless the rider has fallen into water and risks drowning, do NOT move him. Wait for paramedics, who can minimize further damage in case of a bone fracture or spinal-cord injury. Do not remove the rider's helmet or hat in most cases.

■ If the rider is unconscious, make sure he's breathing and that he has a clear airway and a pulse. If necessary, start CPR.

■ If the rider is conscious, ask him if he is able to move his arms and legs. If he can't, or is in pain, help him stay calm while you wait for help. Provide shade from the sun or warmth from the cold.

■ Even if the rider appears uninjured, ask a few simple questions to check for mental clarity. Confusion or short-term memory loss may indicate a concussion. If the rider seems dazed, do not allow him to remount the horse.

Away from home

Let's say you and a friend are out on a trail ride with no cellular phone and your friend falls and is injured. Do you stay with your friend, or go for help? If he's unconscious, stay with him — if he "wakes up" and stumbles off on his own, he could end up lost, on top of being seriously injured.

If he's conscious but confused, and if his other injuries can be stabilized (for instance, by wrapping a sprained/fractured ankle to immobilize it), put him on the calmest horse, and lead or pony him slowly to help. However, if he's lucid and agrees to stay put and wait for your return, go for help alone to minimize further injury and to speed getting assistance. Be sure you know where you are so you can direct help to the site.

Of course, says Dr. Hammett, several precautions taken beforehand can help reduce — or even prevent— fall-related injuries. Her recommendations:

■ Riders should wear an ASTM/SEI-certified riding helmet, as well as appropriate footwear (a shoe that covers the ankle, with an elevated heel — no tennis shoes!).

■ Riders should know to tuck and roll during a fall, not try to "catch" themselves with an outstretched arm.

■ Riders should have sufficient riding instruction (at least 40 hours, according to the American Association of Horsemanship Safety) before heading out on the trail, and should be on horses suited to their ability.

■ Wherever you ride, carry a portable phone (and know the appropriate local phone number for emergencies). Be sure that someone back at the barn knows where you're going and what time to expect you back. ■PH■

For more information, contact:
American Medical Equestrian Assn.
502-695-8940
www.law.utexas.edu/dawson/amea

Our thanks to contributing writer Liz Nutter

Notes

22

Cooling Out

*Cooling out is the process of helping your horse's body
return to his normal resting state after exercise.
This includes more than just
bringing down his body temperature.*

Why does the horse need special attention after exercise? After all, exercise is a normal part of life, and the horse is generally considered to be an athletic animal, well suited to work. Is all of this "cooling out" stuff making a big deal out of nothing, especially in cooler weather?

Not really. Yes, the horse is basically suited to work, being a beast of burden for centuries. But we work and keep our horses in a manner different from how they would behave and exercise in their natural state. For one thing, wild horses travel at a steady, usually slow, pace. The dramatic footage you see in the movies of bands of wild horses moving at a flat gallop across the plains is Hollywood's conception of what would look dramatic, romantic and appealing. Unless the horses are being chased (maybe by those cameramen in helicopters), they are more likely to be found grazing, walking or moving at a steady trot.

Although the wild horse's pace is more energy conserving, he gets a lot of conditioning. Roaming the ranges all day, instead of being confined to a stall or limited area, results in strong muscles, bones, tendons and ligaments and a cardiovascular fitness that is difficult, if not impossible, to achieve under domestic conditions.

Therefore, reason number one why the horse needs special care and cooling out is that **domestic horses can't build and maintain the natural strength and fitness achieved under natural conditions in the wild.**

Allow 10 to 15 minutes walking at the end of your ride to begin the cooling-out process.

Taking our wild horse example a little further, you would not see a band of horses going for a brisk one-hour session of work up and down hills, cantering, cutting, jumping or similar moderate-to-heavy level of exertion, then heading for the nearest water hole, drinking their fill and plopping to the ground for a snooze! If anything happens to cause these horses to really exert themselves, they will slow down when they feel the immediate danger has passed, but remain vigilant and somewhat agitated for a while, slowing the pace but remaining on the move. Thus they catch their breath as they continue to mill about. Eating or drinking only occurs in quick bites or gulps, with the horses remaining alert to possible danger again for quite some time. This allows for a gradual return to normal temperature, pulse and respiration.

The effects of exercise

When a horse exercises, dramatic changes take place in his body. His heart rate elevates (up to greater than 200 with extreme exertion), breathing rate increases, and blood flow shifts away from internal organs not essential to exercise (the brain and heart remain well supplied, but the intestinal tract and kidneys are not) and centers on the working muscles.

As the horse heats up, blood flow to the skin increases, again at the expense of internal organs. The horse's metabolism greatly speeds up to generate the needed energy for exercise. Hormonal changes occur both during and after exercise. Electrolyte patterns shift in the exercising muscle and in the blood. Tendons are repeatedly lengthened and shortened, and the joints are put through various ranges of motion. Even the nervous system gets a workout.

Exercise also generates a tremendous amount of heat, which the horse must get rid of to avoid damaging his internal organs and brain. Waste products, such as lactic acid build-up in the muscles and the blood, must be excreted. The horse loses fluids, both in sweat and by evaporation along the respiratory tract. Electrolytes are lost in sweat and in urine if exercise is prolonged.

Failure of the horse to return to his normal resting state as quickly as possible can result in dehydration, overheating or heat stroke, metabolic abnormalities and cramping of the muscles.

A DRY COAT IS NOT A RELIABLE INDICATOR THAT THE HORSE HAS COOLED OUT, ESPECIALLY IF THE HUMIDITY IS LOW.

Bathing to cool down

Proper cooling out begins before you dismount. A 10- to 15-minute walking period at the end of an exercise session is the best start. **By keeping the horse moving at a slow pace, you maintain blood flow to the muscles, which helps assure that all waste products get flushed out of the muscle tissue.** The blood returning to the muscles will be rich in oxygen, glucose and electrolytes to replenish the muscle cells and to let the muscles relax.

This slow walking also begins the process of bringing the heart rate back to a normal level. Blood begins to be redistributed back to the intestinal tract, liver and kidneys. The liver and kidneys then assist in the processing of wastes from exercise, and intestinal tract function returns to more normal levels.

Sweating will decrease as the pace is slowed, and breathing will slow. By allowing the horse this time of slow walking before you dismount, untack and give him a bath, you help avoid muscle cramping, which can result when exercise stops suddenly.

After walking under saddle, bring the horse in, remove all tack and give him a bath. Plain water is fine. You can also use one of the many liniments or braces designed for use after exercise. These cut through grease and sweat and open the pores. **Heat is transferred from the horse to the bath water, so you'll want to either continue running water over the horse for a few minutes while he cools or scrape the hot water off him so evaporation can aid the cooling process.** Ingredients such as witch hazel and alcohol also help the horse to cool out quicker since they evaporate readily.

If he seems very hot or stressed, take the horse's temperature before giving the bath. **Temperatures in the 105° range mean the horse is in danger of heat stroke.** Hose him with liberal amounts of cold water until his temperature comes down to 103° or lower.

Check the horse's respiratory rate also (count the number of breaths per minute). An upper-normal range is about 16 to 18. **The more overheated/distressed the horse is, the higher his respiratory rate will be.** Horses who are obviously working hard (heaving to breathe), with temperature elevated in the danger zone, should be hosed until they become more comfortable. If no improvement is seen within five minutes, call the veterinarian immediately.

You may have heard it is not a good idea to hose the large muscles of the hindquarters with cold water as this could produce cramping or tying-up. Controlled studies found no evidence this is true. Common sense tells you to use water that is cool/tepid rather than icy unless the horse is dangerously overheated (105° or over), simply to avoid having sensitive horses "scrunch down" and tuck their tails when you hose them.

Therefore, except for comfort, there is little reason to be worried about using cold water on the hind end. An exception to this might be a horse who is already crampy/tight over the hindquarters after work. You still want the muscles to cool down, but you don't want the horse to contract them further in response to the water. Tepid water will relax the horse, hasten cooling and allow circulation to continue, washing out the metabolic wastes from the muscle.

You may also have heard that you should always hose off the legs of the horse first. There is no practical reason to do this. The horse will cool by evaporation, conduction and convection from all body surface areas equally well. To help cool the interior of the horse more quickly, apply ice or cold water over the groove in the neck where the large jugular vein runs. This carries cooled blood directly to the lungs and heart.

For horses who are jumpy, sensitive to water temperature or object in general to being hosed, hosing the legs first may be preferred.

Once the horse has stopped fidgeting and has accepted having his legs hosed, you can gradually work upward to the upper limbs and then the body and head.

The pinch test

Remember the commercial for breakfast cereal that advised you to try to "pinch an inch" to see if you were carrying too much weight? A variation of this can be used as a quick way to gauge if your horse is dehydrated. Pick up a fold of skin on the horse's neck between your thumb and fingers, pulling it away from the muscle underneath to form a "tent." When you let go, the skin should quickly

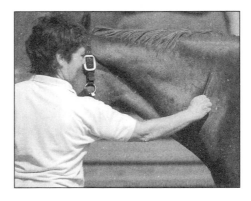

return to its flat, normal position. If it remains tented up, the horse is probably dehydrated. (An exception to this is older horses where the elasticity of the skin is poor.) Another good indicator of hydration is to insert your finger into the horse's mouth. The tongue and gums should feel slightly moist and smooth. If they are sticky or "tacky," the horse is likely dehydrated.

Continued cooling out

After bathing, scrape off all excess water and offer the horse a drink. **Allow the horse to drink freely but no more than half a bucket (two gallons) of water at a time.** Since a hot horse does not have normal gastrointestinal function, too much water may give him a bellyache. On the other hand, the water will be absorbed and passed through to the intestinal tract quickly if the horse has an empty stomach, so it is safe to allow consumption of up to a gallon or so of water every five to 10 minutes until the horse has had his fill.

After the first drink of water, begin walking the horse in a cool and shaded area. The horse should NOT be blanketed unless the air temperature is low enough to cause shivering. Blanketing slows the cooling-out process. (An exception to this might be a horse who is obviously experiencing cramping in the hindquarters. Massage and cover the area with a towel or light blanket to encourage blood flow during cooling out and help relieve the cramping.)

Antisweat sheets are mesh blankets for cooling out in hot weather. They allow the heat to escape (instead of trapping it as other blankets do) and don't promote sweating. These sheets work well, but no better than a regular fly sheet, which also allows efficient heat escape while providing protection from insects.

The observant rider may note an interesting phenomenon at five to 15 minutes after exercise has stopped: The horse seems to get hot again. The horse may have seemed fairly comfortable, with respiratory rate coming down nicely, but he then begins to breathe more rapidly. This is probably related to the muscles "dumping" a load of waste products into the blood at this time and is most often seen when horses have worked very hard and work was stopped suddenly without a cool-down under saddle.

Continue cooling the horse but keep an eye on the respiratory rate. It should fall again fairly quickly as you continue walking. If it does not, recheck the horse's temperature — he may need hosing again. If his temperature has not gone up again, check for a cause of pain, such as a cramped muscle or pulled tendon.

A common mistake is putting the horse away too soon. **A dry coat is NOT a reliable indicator that the horse has cooled out, especially if the humidity is low.** Putting the horse into the stall too quickly may result in him sweating and even blowing again (the first from heat, the second from unresolved metabolic abnormalities as well as heat).

A light fly sheet will allow sweat to evaporate.

A better indicator is the horse's temperature. Temperature should be 101° or lower before you put the horse away in a stall and leave him. He should also have had his fill of water and be interested in eating by this time. A horse whose coat has dried, whose body and ears feel cool to the touch (ears will always feel cool if the horse has been cooled out properly), has had his fill of water and has a temperature in the range of 101° to 102° can be safely turned out to continue his cooling out.

Cool-weather cooling out

Long-haired horses can be difficult to cool out in cold weather. The dense coat is designed to hold body heat, and it takes a considerable amount of time to dry. After a hard workout where the horse has become sweaty and wet, take him to an area protected from drafts and sponge him down with warm water with a good body wash (not soap) added. The body wash will cut through dirt, sweat and grease, making drying the horse much easier. Scrape off the excess, then towel the horse vigorously, fluffing up all the hair to expose the undercoat. The horse should then be covered with a cooler and walked until the cooler's surface becomes covered with moisture.

At this point, drying can be hastened by removing the cooler, toweling the horse again and putting on a clean, dry cooler. If your horse tends to get an extremely heavy coat, you might want to consider a synthetic-fiber cooler instead of wool. Synthetics allow more rapid evaporation of water.

Some people use two coolers at the same time, especially in cold weather. This is probably not advisable, however, if your horse has developed a winter coat. Two coolers may prevent proper cooling out and drying of the coat.

A horse with a good coat, one cooler and being walked should remain quite comfortable, especially if he's protected from direct winds. Let common sense be your guide. If the horse is shivering, put on another cooler. Otherwise, the job will be done much more efficiently by following the guidelines above for toweling and changing coolers.

Care after cooling out

When is it safe to feed a horse after exercise? Horses may become interested in eating before the circulation to their stomach and intestines has completely returned to normal. Unrestricted eating at this time can cause anything from mild abdominal discomfort to obvious colic, even founder.

It is fine to allow the horse some grazing during cooling out (as long as he has stopped "blowing" and sweating and his temperature is coming down). Once the horse has been cooled out using the guidelines described, put him back in his stall or corral and observe him for 10 to 15 minutes. If he still appears to be normal, he can be safely given about five pounds of hay. Grain is another story, though. **It is a good idea to always wait a minimum of a full hour after the horse has been put away to provide a grain meal.**

From a balanced diet, horses can replace most, if not all, of the electrolytes they lose, especially if they are not worked heavily every day. Horses who are working regularly in hot weather, however, or horses who tend to become dehydrated easily or who have a tendency toward any muscle soreness, may benefit from electrolyte supplementation.

Finally, after an exercise session, check the horse's legs and muscles. Lamenesses, swelling of tendons and ligaments, even muscle soreness may take hours to appear or to be bad enough that you notice it. Run your hands down the legs, beginning at knees/hocks and progressing to the hooves. Check that they feel cool, with no swelling, and that all legs and hooves feel the same temperature.

Exert gentle pressure with your fingertips along the muscles of the back and rump. If not tender, the horse will show no reaction (with allowances made for individual temperaments!). If tender, the horse will flinch, tighten up or sink down away from the pressure; he may even kick. If there's a significant problem, call the veterinarian for advice. If an area seems suspicious, but the horse is generally comfortable, make a mental note to check him again later on. ▣

23

What Keeps Us Safe?

Body protectors, safety helmets, break-away stirrups
and even round pens. What do they have in common?
They are all designed to keep us safe.
But can we rely on them?

Imagine that you bought a limousine equipped with all the best safety features, from side-impact airbags and anti-lock brakes to super-duper bumpers. You're ready for your first drive, but your chauffeur shows up for work totally drunk. Will you be safe on the highway? No. Why not? Because the driver can't control the vehicle.

If you decided that factor wasn't important, and you put your confidence in the safety equipment on your vehicle, what's likely to happen out on the road? A scary ride, and perhaps a wreck.

Let's say that you make it home safely after one drive, but day after day the driver shows up in the same condition. Sooner or later, you are going to have a major wreck and maybe injure someone else as well. While no sensible person would get in that limo, countless riders do the equivalent — they trust their safety to equipment instead of control.

Safety equipment

Take, for instance, items such as tie-downs, martingales, draw reins and the like. Such devices are designed to prevent a horse from throwing his head (possibly hitting the rider's head with his) or to limit the range of movement of the horse's head. And they work fine until the horse's desire to move his head, possibly even involuntarily as

What keeps this knight safe? Certainly not the body armor. It's her control of her horse.

he nips at a fly or as he spooks, is greater than his desire to avoid pressure from those devices. Then something gives. Either the horse's front feet come off the ground or the horse "fights" the restraint, requiring heavier-duty restraints to achieve the desired effect.

How about outfitting the rider for safety? Sure. You can begin with a helmet, then boots and a body protector vest. Add safety stirrups, and the rider is assured of a safe ride. Right? Not necessarily.

The only thing that keeps a rider safe is controlling his horse. That said, there's nothing wrong with safety equipment — in fact, using it is an excellent idea. The job of safety gear, however, is to minimize damage in case of a wreck. It doesn't prevent a wreck, so it can't keep you truly safe.

Environmental controls

Is it important to control the environment in which you work your horse? You bet. That's why we work horses in a round pen — because it's the safest classroom in which to begin teaching your horse. **The more the horse is out of control, the more important it is to control the environment.** Yet, both you and your horse certainly can get hurt in the round pen. Will controlling the environment keep you safe? In a few circumstances, maybe, but you can't depend on environmental control to safeguard your well-being.

For instance, I meet show-ring riders who blame their horse's poor performance on a distraction near the arena, and trail riders who blame another horse for their own horse going too fast. They even blame the horse back home who calls to the one they are riding, or they blame the farmer down the street who brought in new cattle. The crowd, buddy horse or cows aren't the problem — the actual danger lies in the fact that the rider didn't have the horse sufficiently trained.

How about the rider who gets kicked by another rider's horse? It would be easy to blame the other rider or horse. But, in truth, we want our horse to be so responsive to our cues that should a threat like that appear, we can move him out of the other's kicking range — and now!

So what should you do? Train your horse. Develop such good control that you can control your horse's feet, regardless of the distraction. It's following safe training principles and gaining control of the horse that will keep you out of harm's way.

So, how do you stay safe?

■ *Operate from a position of control. Make up your mind that you will not do anything with the horse that allows him to be in control — and you, consequently, out of control. This means you can't assume that you are in control — you must learn to recognize when the horse is essentially out of control. For instance, when he rushes out of the stall instead of respecting your lead rope cues, imagine riding that same horse on a trail ride and having the other horses ride away. Who would be in control then?*

■ *Follow the three rules — that you can't get hurt, the horse can't get hurt, and the horse should be calmer at the end of the lesson than at the beginning — in deciding what training method to follow.*

■ *Train all three parts of the horse — mental, physical and emotional. That means every third lesson you should focus on training your horse's emotions. It won't help you to train him to a cue if he doesn't obey that cue when he gets excited.*

■ *Ride where you can, not where you can't. If you can't control your horse's speed on the trail, ride him where you can control his speed and work on speed-control exercises. For instance, I don't ask my horse to do any exercise on the trail that I haven't worked on at home.*

■ *The horse's attention is the last thing you'll get.* *First comes the rider's concentration, then the rider's consistent performance, then the horse's concentration. Then, when his performance is consistent, we finally get his attention. But, we really don't care about his attention — we care about his performance.*

■ *The more steps in the lesson plan, the faster the training goes.* *The bigger the step you ask your horse to make, the greater the risk of failure. But if you essentially only ask questions that he can answer "yes" to, you won't have a problem with a giant "NO" at the wrong time. Challenge yourself to put as many steps in the training as you can think of — and you'll be amazed at your horse's progress.*

■ *Your horse is your horse.* *Don't let anyone pressure you into doing something with your horse that you don't feel comfortable doing. For instance, if you don't feel*

There isn't a tie-down or head-down device that can control the elevation of a horse's head like the rider's hands on the reins can. The horse who throws his head or rears doesn't need a tie-down — he needs to learn the "calm down" cue.

safe crossing the creek, don't cross the creek. Instead, work on control exercises until your horse is trained well enough that he can obey your cues despite the distraction of a creek.

When preparing to load your horse into the trailer, don't pressure him into the trailer — no matter how helpful other people want to be.

Buying stuff

So, is safety equipment worth buying? In many cases, yes, because you want to do everything you can, not just to avoid a wreck, but to limit the chance for injury or even pain.

For instance, when I start an "unbroke" horse in the round pen, I always put leg protection on him, because I can't control his movements. Once I can control his feet, then leg protection is less critical.

When I ride the horse, asking him to do maneuvers in which he may hit one leg with another, such as working on lead changes, I make sure to use leg protection on the horse. I don't want the horse to feel any pain. If he hits his leg once or twice, he'll be afraid of making the same mistake again, so he'll be less likely to find the right option.

How about helmets for riders? I highly recommend them. There's always the possibility that you may fall off even a horse who is under control — and a helmet protects the head.

Leg wraps and other forms of protection are always a good idea.

We don't have to wait until we are injured before we know we're not in control. And, we shouldn't deny reality by relying only on equipment. Like seat belts in a car, equipment or environment offers some protection if you wreck, but it doesn't prevent the wreck. The only way to prevent a wreck is to control your horse. Control keeps you safe. ▣

Notes

Index

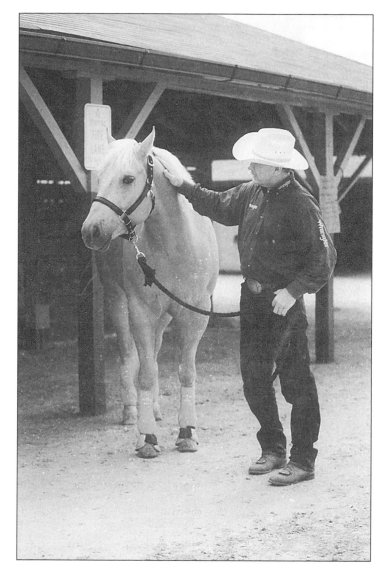

For information regarding *John Lyons' Perfect Horse*,
the monthly magazine, or other books in the John Lyons Perfect
Horse Library, see our web site www.perfecthorse.com
or call the publisher, Belvoir Publications, Inc. at 800-424-7887.

PHOTO CREDITS: MAUREEN GALLATIN, CHARLES HILTON, LIZ NUTTER,
SUE STUSKA, MARK WALPIN, KAY WHITTINGTON
BOOK DESIGN AND LAYOUT: SUSAN R. TOMKIN